Activities, Guidelines, and Resources for
TEACHERS OF SPECIAL LEARNERS

Activities, Guidelines, and Resources for
TEACHERS OF SPECIAL LEARNERS

Carol A. Cartwright
G. Phillip Cartwright
The Pennsylvania State University

Marjorie Ward
The Ohio State University

Sara Willoughby-Herb
Clarion State College

Wadsworth Publishing Company
Belmont, California
A Division of Wadsworth, Inc.

Education Editor: Marshall Aronson
Production Editor: Carolyn Tanner
Copy Editor: Carol Dondrea
Illustrator: Virginia Mickelson

Cover art: Morris Louis. Point of Tranquility. 1958. Acrylic on canvas,
8'5 3/8" x 11'3". Collection: The Hirshhorn Museum and Sculpture Garden,
Smithsonian Institution. Photo by John Tennant.

Photo credits: p. 250

Printed in the United States of America

1 2 3 4 5 6 7 8 9 10---85 84 83 82 81

ISBN 0-534-00940-9

Contents

About the Book

The activities and resources in this book are a collection of individual and group activities, together with comprehensive lists of print and nonprint resources, designed for your use in furthering understanding of exceptional children and the educational services they require.

Most of the ideas presented have been tested—by the authors, by their students, or by teachers across the nation. A variety of activities has been included because some teachers will find certain kinds of activities more helpful than others. Also, our experience has shown us that teachers need to have many different activities available in order to meet the varying needs of exceptional children.

The material in the book is organized in three parts. Part One, Understanding Exceptionalities, includes suggestions and activities intended to develop sensitivity and understanding of the problems typically experienced by exceptional individuals.

Part Two, Working with Children in the Mainstream, is a collection of activities to be used in gaining and extending skills needed to work successfully with exceptional children. The emphasis is on accommodating the children in the least restrictive, most nearly normal, situation possible. For many exceptional children, this will mean a public school setting. Activities to sharpen skills in cooperating with other professionals and parents are also included in Part Two.

Part Three includes extensive lists of resources: films and other media; books for professionals, parents, and children; names and addresses of manufacturers, distributors, and publishers of special equipment and materials; and names and addresses of professional organizations and advocacy groups. It might be said that just about everything you always wanted to know about special education can be found by consulting one or more of the resources listed in Part Three.

Teachers who work with either exceptional or nonhandicapped children will find the activities useful. Most of the activities have been designed so they can be either used as part of group projects or completed independently by a single person. Each activity can stand alone in the sense that it can be completed without having completed other activities in the handbook. Also, activities can be used in a different sequence from that which we have used since one activity is not a prerequisite to others.

This book is an ideal accompaniment to an introductory textbook in special education such as Cartwright, Cartwright, and Ward, <u>Educating Special Learners</u> (Wadsworth, 1981). It provides hands-on activities that help in bridging theory and abstract information and practice. The book will also be welcomed by in-service teachers who are interested in self-directed learning activities and independent study projects that will help them review and become revitalized.

Acknowledgments

We express our appreciation to the following Penn State graduate students who assisted us in locating and documenting resources: Bo In Chung, Elizabeth Hrncir, Chris Richardson, Cecelia Ward, and Marci Weiner. Several typists helped at one point or another in the preparation of the manuscript; we extend our thanks to Betty Ayers, Jean Dale, JoAnn Dreibelbis, Gloria Sampsell, and Anna Simco. All of the activities have been field tested by students in our College courses or by teachers working with us on inservice projects. We appreciate their generosity, honesty, and spontaneity in suggesting revisions.

To Our Children

Catherine, Stephen, and Susan Cartwright
Anne Forsberg
Maggie Willoughby-Herb

Activities, Guidelines, and Resources for
TEACHERS OF SPECIAL LEARNERS

Part One:

Understanding Exceptionalities

Introduction to Part One

As teachers, we often describe and label children's behavior as abnormal, delayed, retarded, deviant, and so on. The use of such labels accentuates differences among children. When we think of children as being different, we begin to treat them differently, and perhaps have different expectations of them. This kind of treatment by teachers, in turn, may influence children's self-concepts so that they behave in a more deviant manner than they would have if the treatment had been more normal.

We must train ourselves to view exceptional persons not as different per se, but as persons who manifest certain behaviors that range more or less from the norm. By observing the significant behavior characteristics of both normal and exceptional children within our classrooms we can improve our ability to detect and understand the individual differences exhibited by all people. For example, if we are concerned about a child who is inattentive, we should refrain from judging whether the child "has a problem" until we also know the normal attending behaviors of children in the classroom. In collecting data on attention for both normal and exceptional children in the classroom, we usually see that most children benefit from instruction in attending skills.

The activities in Part One, Understanding Exceptionalities, are designed to make you more aware of the problems experienced by exceptional persons and their families. You will have opportunities to explore your attitudes toward those who are exceptional. You will see that some of the activities could be used to help others, including elementary school children, develop more positive attitudes toward exceptional persons.

Activities

Problem Behaviors and Classroom Norms

Observation is a powerful tool in studying human behavior. Teachers who are just beginning to explore the potential of observation are usually surprised to learn that the hard facts (the data gained through careful observation) about children in their classrooms are often different from the generalizations they carry around in their heads. This is so because we are human and subject to forgetfulness and personal biases. In other words, we tend to see what we want to see rather than what is really there.

Teachers who make careful observation a habit are in a good position to understand the range of individual differences in their classrooms and to make more valid judgments about which behaviors of which children are significant deviations from normal. Prove this to yourself with the following activity.

Observe a significant behavior characteristic (talking out, lack of responsiveness, verbal or physical aggression, inattention, and so on) of children in a mainstreamed class. Make sure you sample carefully so that the children you select for observation are representative of the entire class and include children identified as exceptional as well as normal. Concentrate on a single behavior. Use whatever aids are appropriate to make the observations efficient and unobtrusive. For example, if you are observing instances of physical aggression you might wear a wrist counter like those worn by golfers to keep track of their strokes on the golf course. Each day for three weeks you might count the instances of physical aggression for a different child in the group. When your observations are completed, compare your findings for all the children you have observed. What is the norm (average frequency) for that behavior within the classroom? What is the range of that behavior in the group: Who exhibited the behavior the most and who the least? How does the behavior of the exceptional child or children compare with the behavior of classmates? Did an exceptional child exhibit that behavior the most or the least? What does your experience tell you about the importance of knowing classroom norms before deciding that a child has a problem?

Social Acceptance of Deviancy

In order to enhance the normalization of handicapped persons, our society must accept deviancy and broaden its notions concerning normal ranges of behavior. For example, if all persons in our society were aware of the prevalence and nature of various crippling conditions, they would be able to react to persons having such disorders in a more natural manner—rather than behaving uncomfortably, or even rudely.

We can assess society's acceptance of deviancy in many ways, including through the media. Spend a period of time watching television or reading newspapers, magazines, or comic books. Note the frequency with which handicapped persons appear and how the handicapping condition is depicted. What does your observation tell you about our society's treatment of deviancy?

Teaching Children to Accept Deviancy

We can broaden children's perspectives on ranges of normative behavior by exposing them to models possessing a range of deviant behaviors. For example, we might occasionally use wall posters depicting blind persons, the physically handicapped, and so on. We might choose literature in which the main or supporting characters are handicapped.

Find out what kinds of materials are available to assist teachers in presenting a range of models. Look at several teaching materials catalogs or children's literature books and record your findings. What is your assessment of the availability of such materials? What are your recommendations for improving available materials, so that they portray the handicapped more accurately?

Common Reactions to Exceptional Persons

Common situations are made more difficult and stressful for the exceptional person because of others' reactions to him or her. Try assuming a handicapping condition for a period of time. Speech defects are fairly easy to assume. Or you might be able to borrow a wheelchair, a hearing aid, dark glasses and cane, and so on. Choose an activity that will force you to interact with as many people as possible. You might take a bus into town for a shopping trip, for example. Record how people reacted to you and how you, in turn, adjusted your behavior to their reactions.

If possible, try to do this activity with a partner. While one person assumes a handicapping condition, the other person can be the observer. Then you can exchange roles and do the activity a second time.

Overcoming Stereotypes

Too often parents and teachers fall into the practice of imposing stereotypes on handicapped children. Here is an activity that you can use yourself or

with parents to help focus on a child's individuality. Try the activity yourself, using a handicapped child you know or have observed.*

First, study the drawing labeled "Stereotypes Associated with Handicapped
Children" on p. 6. Then, think about the child you know. Try to see the child's
individuality. Fill out the blank form on p. 7, noting the child's unique characteristics instead of the stereotypes. Later, think about or discuss these
questions:

1. Do you think many persons impose stereotypes on the handicapped child?
Who are they and what adverse effects can this have on a child?

2. How can we help ourselves and others see our children as individuals
instead of stereotyping them as handicapped persons?

Daily Routines Influenced by Handicapping Conditions

On the chart on p. 8, fill in the left-hand column by listing all your morning
or afternoon activities. Be as specific as possible. Then, randomly select one
of these handicapping conditions: deafness, blindness, physical disability
(specify), speech impairment, mental retardation. In the second column list
all the difficulties you would have in performing those routines if you had
that handicapping condition. In the third column indicate any ways in which
your handicapping condition might enhance or strengthen the performance of
these routines.

Discuss your responses with classmates or colleagues, if possible. What should
be your responsibilities, as teachers, for helping the exceptional child cope
with daily routines?

*Adapted from Jenkins and Macdonald, Growing Up Equal, © 1979. Reprinted by
 permission of Prentice-Hall, Inc., Englewood Cliffs, New Jersey.

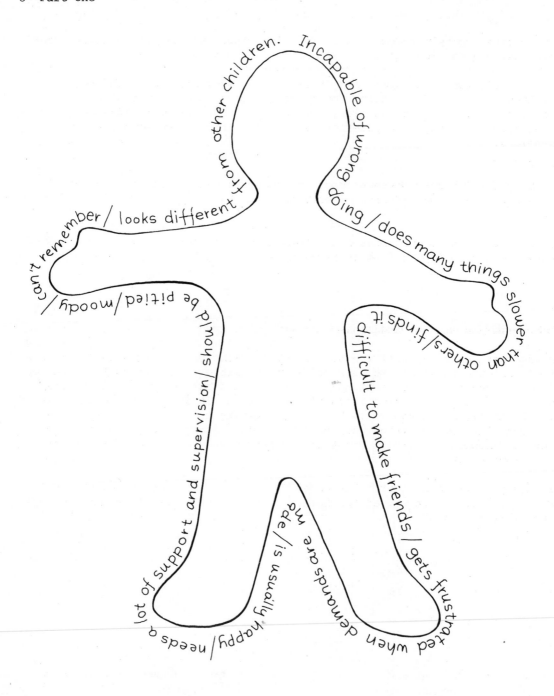

Stereotypes Associated with Handicapped Children

Handicapping condition: _____

Routines/Activities	Difficulties	Strengths

The Exceptional Child's Frustrations in School

Some of us have experienced situations in which we were less capable than most of our peers. Perhaps we were not skilled at a particular sport, or had difficulty learning a foreign language. The distress we felt at those times is a mere approximation of the frustrations faced by many exceptional children throughout the school day. Divide your class into groups of five or six and try to pinpoint some of these frustrations by role-playing the following situation. If you are not in a class, try to observe a lesson such as the one described.

Assign one group member to be the teacher, another to be an exceptional student (with a severe visual or auditory impairment), and the rest to be normal students. Have the teacher conduct a 10- or 15-minute lesson appropriate for a grade level chosen by the group. Choose a lesson that involves both teacher instruction and pupil participation. At the end of the lesson discuss these questions.

1. What types of information were available to the normal children, but not to the exceptional child? How important was this information?
2. How much positive (smiles, praise) and negative (corrections, frowns) feedback was available to the regular children vs. the exceptional child?
3. Did the teacher use any concepts that were difficult for the exceptional child to comprehend?
4. Review all tasks that the children were asked to perform (e.g., attending to various stimuli, answering). What proportion of these were reasonably attainable by the exceptional child?
5. How would repeated experiences such as this lesson probably affect the exceptional child's self-concept (viewing himself or herself in terms of cognitive and affective concerns)?

The Gifted Child's Frustrations in School

Many teachers find the gifted child especially difficult to teach since these children are not often motivated in the same ways as their classmates. They are often already familiar with, or just uninterested in, the curriculum. In order to understand how these gifted children may be feeling during a normal school day, let's analyze some similar experiences of our own. On the form on the next page, list the three most boring situations you've been in during the past month. Try to identify what made the situations boring. Finally, tell how you reacted to being in those situations.

After you complete the chart, think about what you have written and how it applies to teaching. Are any of the causes for your own boredom similar to children's classroom experiences? Do your reactions provide any clues for better understanding children's behavior? Do your personal experiences give you ideas about preventing boredom in children? How?

Boring situations	Caused boredom	How I reacted

Self-Concept Development and the Handicapped Child

When children go to school they engage in many activities that contribute to their self-awareness. They learn which aspects of the environment they can and can't control, they receive positive or negative feedback as they interact socially, and they master certain skills and struggle or fail at others.

Observe a handicapped and a normal child during part of a classroom day. Notice how various aspects of their activities contribute to the children's self-concept development. Record your observations in the following chart. What differences in outcomes do you see for the two children? How are school activities detrimental and beneficial to the self-concept development of handicapped children?

	Activity descriptions	Possible influence on self-concept
Child 1		
Child 2		

Community Services for the Handicapped

Researchers at the University of Washington* conducted a community survey to
identify the kinds and extent of community services available to severely and
profoundly handicapped persons. They investigated services such as medical
care, dental care, child care, insurance, religion, restaurants, and transportation. In their survey, they asked questions such as whether those services were willing to treat severely handicapped persons, whether they made
referrals to agencies that would provide treatment, whether special programs
were available for the handicapped, whether their facilities provided access
to handicapped services, and so on. The researchers found that few services
were equally available to the handicapped and the nonhandicapped.

Design and conduct a survey in your community similar to the one just described. You might want to focus on community services available to a particular age group such as preschoolers or adolescents, or to those who have a
particular handicapping condition—for example, the physically disabled. Report your findings to the class, if possible, discussing their implications
for handicapped persons, their families, and for educators and other human
service professionals.

Describing Teachers' Roles

Interview a regular and a special class teacher who teach at approximately the
same grade level. Write a job description for each of them, based on your interview. Use the form on the next page. What tasks and skills are common to
both professionals? In what way do their jobs differ? What skills and attributes do you think are especially important for those persons who wish to work
with exceptional children?

*L. A. Kenowitz; J. Gallagher; and E. Edgar, "Generic Services for the Se-
verely Handicapped and Their Families: What's Available?" In Educational
Programming for the Severely and Profoundly Handicapped, ed. E. Sontag,
Reston, Va.: Council for Exceptional Children, 1977.

Job description: Regular education teacher	Job description: Special education teacher

Experiencing Handicaps

The article excerpted below* describes an "aging kit" devised by E. D. Glover, a professor at Texas Christian University, to give people experience with some of the problems of old age. After reading the article, note how you could apply similar techniques to help yourself, children, or adults understand certain handicapping conditions. Could you put together a similar kit on handicapping conditions? What kinds of activities and follow-up experiences would make the activity most worthwhile?

With the help of Mr. Glover's kit, student Beth Levine ages about seventy years in a few minutes. Here's how the handicaps were produced:

*Loss of hearing: Ms. Levine stuffed cotton balls in her ears and put on ear muffs. She then tried to converse with someone across the room.

*Loss of sight: Ms. Levine put on glasses covered with crumpled cellophane, then tried to read and thread a needle.

*Loss of smell and taste; difficulty in breathing: She placed cotton balls in her nostrils and then ate a slice of apple. It was virtually tasteless. Later, with her chest wrapped tightly with a four-inch elastic bandage and the cotton balls still in place, she tried to breathe through a straw.

*Loss of touch: Ms. Levine donned heavy gloves. (Coating the fingers with rubber cement produces the same effect.) She then tried to perform simple tasks such as threading a needle, buttoning a coat, and picking up coins from a table top.

*Loss of mobility: She wrapped bandages around her knees and elbows and tried to walk and to climb stairs.

Back in her twenties, Ms. Levine reflects on the experience: "It took effort to move, and just breathing was a strain. It wore me out to cross the room." She says she found that her deafness and blindness tended to isolate her.

*From The Chronicle of Higher Education, June 25, 1979. Reprinted by permission.

Part Two:

Working with Children in the Mainstream

Introduction to Part Two

Being sensitive to the special needs of exceptional youngsters is part of the story but not all of it. In addition to being aware of special needs and knowledgeable about groups of exceptional children, you need skills to work with these children and their families. Part Two includes group and individual projects that will help you test your current skills and develop new ones. Some people will say that some of these activities are just "plain good teaching." Perhaps so, but that does not make them any less important—especially since exceptional children have many needs and behaviors in common with other children.

Most of the activities are set up so that you practice applying skills to the special needs of exceptional youngsters. The title, Working with Children in the Mainstream, indicates that the general focus of the activities is working with exceptional people in the least restrictive environment—for many, that will be the regular public school. Part Two begins with a section called Assessment, since assessment skills are needed to identify the children who need special help. Skills in assessing programs and environments as well as children are included. Another section, called Generic Teaching Skills, includes ideas on how to adapt general teaching skills to special groups. The section entitled Curricular Adjustments helps you see how to modify content for various disability groups. The sections called Writing Individualized Education Programs (IEPs) and Tips on Integrating Handicapped Children should be especially useful because the skills they present are pivotal in making mainstreaming work. Many handicapped children do not need curriculum or methods adjustments, but they do need an adapted environment so they can function in normal situations; therefore a section on adapting environments, Environmental Arrangements, is included. Anyone who has worked with exceptional youngsters will tell you that it is a team effort. We agree wholeheartedly and, to complete Part Two, have included activities to sharpen your skills in working with other professionals and with parents.

Section A: Assessment

Use of Developmental Checklists for Assessment and Program Planning

Checklists can be built from information about normal child development and used in various ways. Perhaps the most obvious use is for the comprehensive recording of a child's current levels of functioning. By noting which behaviors are present and which are not, we obtain a picture of what a child can do at a given time. If the checklist is used over a period of time for the same child, we can note new behaviors that are acquired and thus create a continuous record of child performance. Program planning can be based on information about what the child already knows and on a consideration of next steps in the developmental sequence.

Developmental checklists also serve to improve understanding of "normal" development. The checklists are constructed from information about the typical performance of children at different ages and stages of development, but after using the checklist once or twice, you will realize that no child falls exactly at the "normal" point on every characteristic listed on the checklist. Thus, we have a graphic reminder of individual differences and the relative nature of normality.

A developmental checklist developed by Joe L. Frost of the University of Texas at Austin is provided on the following pages. The items are sequenced, based on rough averages, as follows:

    Level III: 36 to 48 months (3 to 4 years)
    Level IV: 48 to 60 months (4 to 5 years)
    Level   V: 60 to 72 months (5 to 6 years)

Behaviors that are examples of typical accomplishments for children at each level are included. Specific behaviors on the checklist were chosen because they are frequently observed in young children and are often included in curriculum planning for young children.

Several activities involving use of the developmental checklist are given below. You (or members of your group) can brainstorm many others. Even if you do not work with young children, you can still benefit from the activities since the principles they represent can be transferred to other age groups.

1. Use Part B, Socializing, to design a set of interview questions that can be used as part of the intake information for a preschool program. Try out your interview with several parents and ask for feedback regarding such things as clarity of the questions, ease of response, and appropriateness of the questions.

2.   Observe several children on items included in Part C, Coordinating. Try to include at least two three-year-olds, two four-year-olds, and two five-year-olds in your observations. After recording the observations, write a paragraph about the interindividual differences (differences between children) you observed. Then, choose one child and write a paragraph about that child's intraindividual differences (the pattern of strengths and weaknesses with the child).

3.   Observe one preschool-age child using the entire checklist. Keep a record of the time needed to do the observations. Mark the items that could not be readily observed (i.e., were there tasks that you had to set up specially in advance in order to observe the child's performance? Were there items that you had to ask a teacher about?).

4.   Develop a code that could be used easily with the checklist to record more information than the simple yes-no code (behavior present or absent) now used. Try out the checklist using your code. How does your code work? Could you easily teach it to others?

5.   Choose one part of the checklist (e.g., Part H, Language). Using child development textbooks, published tests, and other sources, develop some items for that part of the checklist for children aged seven, eight, and nine.

6.   If possible, use the checklist to observe an older child who is considered "Developmentally delayed." What conclusions can you draw about the observations?

Developmental Checklists for 3-, 4-, and 5-Year Olds*

A. ATTENDING

Level III						
1. Attends to a story 10-15 minutes						
2. Attends to an activity 15-20 minutes						
3. Repeats parts of stories						
Level IV						
1. Attends to stories and activities						
2. Listens to simple instructions and follows through						
3. Shares short stories with others						
4. Sustained attention span						
Level V						
1. Sustained attention span for a wide variety of activities						

B. SOCIALIZING (Inter- and intrapersonal relationships, play)

Level III						
1. Engages in independent play						
2. Engages in parallel play						
3. Plays briefly with peers						

4. Recognizes needs of others						
5. Shows sympathy for others						
Level IV						
1. Leaves mother readily						
2. Converses with other children						
3. Converses with adults						
4. Plays with peers						
5. Cooperates in classroom routines						
6. Takes turns and shares						
7. Replaces materials after use						
8. Takes care of personal belongings						
9. Respects property of others						
Level V						
1. Cooperates in classroom routines						
2. Completes most self-initiated projects						
3. Replaces materials after use						
4. Takes turns and shares						
5. Takes care of his belongings						
6. Respects others' property						
7. Works and plays with limited supervision						
8. Engages in cooperative play						
9. Listens while peers speak						

10.	Follows multiple and delayed directions					
11.	Carries out special responsibilities (feed animal, etc.)					
12.	Listens and follows suggestions of adult					
13.	Carries out simple errands					
14.	Sensitive to praise and criticism					
15.	Enjoys talking with adults					

C. COORDINATING (Motor, fine and gross, hand-eye, self-help skills)

GROSS MOVEMENT Level III						
1.	Catches ball with both hands against chest					
2.	Walks a balance beam 6 feet					
3.	Hops on both feet several times without assistance					
4.	Throws a ball with accuracy					
5.	Climbs up slide and comes down					
6.	Climbs, alternating feet, holding onto hand rail					
7.	Stands on one foot and balances					
8.	Pushes a loaded wheelbarrow					
9.	Runs freely with little stumbling or falling					
FINE MOVEMENT						
10.	Places small pegs in pegboards					
11.	Holds paintbrush or pencil with whole hand					

12. Cuts with scissors						
13. Uses a knife and fork correctly						
14. Buttons large buttons on own clothes						
15. Puts on coat by self						
16. Strings beads with ease						
17. Hammers a pound toy with accuracy						

GROSS MOVEMENT
Level IV

1. Balances on one foot						
2. Walks on balance beam						
3. Climbs steps with alternate feet						
4. Climbs jungle gym						
5. Can skip haltingly						
6. Rides tricycle						
7. Throws, catches, and bounces large ball						
8. Stacks blocks vertically and horizontally						
9. Creates recognizable block structure						
10. Participates in outdoor play						

FINE MOVEMENT

11. Pounds and rolls clay						
12. Puts together fine-piece puzzle						
13. Forms a pegboard design						
14. Cuts and pastes						

15. Participates in finger plays						
16. Eats with spoon						
17. Holds cup with one hand						
18. Puts coat on hanger or hook						
19. Independent in toileting						
20. Is learning to button buttons, zip zippers, tie shoes						

GROSS MOVEMENT
Level V

1. Catches and throws small ball						
2. Bounces and catches small ball						
3. Can skip						
4. Skips rope						
5. Hops on one foot						
6. Creates tinker toy and block structures						
7. Climbs on jungle gym						
8. Rides tricycle with speed and skill						
9. Hammers and saws with some skill						
10. Can walk a straight line						
11. Descends stairs, alternating feet						

FINE MOVEMENT

12. Cuts and pastes creative designs						
13. Forms variety of pegboard designs						

14. Buttons buttons, zips zippers, ties shoes						
15. Plays jacks						
16. Creates recognizable objects with clay						
17. Independent in toileting						
18. Independent in eating						
19. Independent in dressing and undressing						
20. Learning to tie in out-of-sight locations (under the chin)						
21. Holds and manipulates pencils, crayons, and brushes of various sizes						
22. Combs and brushes hair						

D. RECOGNIZING AND DISCRIMINATING (Identifying—sensory activities)

Level III						
1. Discriminates between two smells						
2. Knows and verbalizes smells are "different"						
3. May be able to label smell or smells (verbally)						
4. Discriminates between two tastes and verbalizes they are "different"						
5. May be able to label taste or tastes (verbally)						
6. Discriminates between two sounds and verbalizes they are "different"						
7. May be able to label sounds (verbally)						

8. Points to different food objects on request					
9. Points to basic shapes (circle, square, triangle) on request					

RECOGNIZING, DISCRIMINATING, CLASSIFYING

Level IV: Uses Multisensory Factors in Learning					
1. Seeing, hearing, tasting, touching, smelling					

2.   Discriminates differences in size and shape of
       concrete objects: big, little, long, short,
       square, round					

3. Classifies objects by weight: heavy, light					
4. Classifies objects by height: tall, short					
5. Identifies primary colors					
6. Discriminates likenesses and differences					
7. Concepts of relative loudness, distance, weight, time judgments					
Level V					

1.   Identifies and labels spatial relationships:
       far/near, in/out, front/back, top/bottom,
       first/last, over/under					

2.   Identifies and discriminates value relationships:
       right/wrong, good/bad, pretty/ugly, sad/happy,
       like/dislike					

3.   Identifies and discriminates value relationships:
       day/night, today/tomorrow, yesterday/today,
       before/after, now/then, earlier/later, never/soon					

4. Identifies primary colors (red, yellow, blue)					
5. Identifies secondary colors (green, orange, purple)					

6. Identifies pastel colors (pink, lavender)						
7. Classifies colors by intensity (dark, light, darker than, lighter than)						
8. Identifies the simple properties of an object						
9. Classifies foods: fruits, vegetables, meats						
10. Classifies tastes: sweet, sour, salty, bitter						
11. Classifies surfaces by texture: smooth, rough, slick, gritty, slimy						
12. Identifies and classifies common objects by shape: circle, square, rectangle, triangle						
13. Classifies objects by more than one property						
14. Seriates objects by size						
15. Seriates sounds by volume						
16. States functions of simple objects						
17. Reverses simple operations						

E.   SYMBOLIZING AND IMITATING

Level III						
1. Recognizes that pictures represent real objects						
2. Draws V or O from model						
3. Imitates grownups (play house, store, etc.)						
4. Imitates "correct behavior"						
5. Expresses frustrations in play						

6. Creates imaginary playmates					
7. Engages in housekeeping					
Level IV					
1. Recognizes likenesses and differences in pictured objects					
2. Role-plays wide variety of roles in housekeeping center and other centers					
3. Role-plays a wide variety of adult occupations					
4. Participates in dramatization of familiar stores					
5. Uses puppets in self-initiated dialogues					
6. Differentiates between real and make-believe					
7. Draws pictures that symbolize events					
8. Tells experiences for an experience story					
9. Draws picture of arranged objects					
10. Draws picture before arranging objects					
Level V					
1. Role-plays in housekeeping and other centers					
2. Role-plays on playground					
3. Role-plays adult occupations					
4. Imitates reading behavior: turns pages front to back, talks about stories, mimics adult reader					

F. CREATIVE EXPRESSION (Exploring, Dramatics, Art, Play)

Level III						
1. Creates new ideas from what he knows						
2. Paints and draws on large paper symbolic figures						
3. Builds simple structures with blocks						
4. Uses transportation toys, people, and animals to enrich block play						
5. Has imaginary companion						
6. Uses puppets to approach others						
7. Imagines any object into the object desired (symbolic function)						
8. Sings simple songs						
Level IV						
1. Pretends dolls are real people						
2. Engages in rhythmic activities						
3. Sings alone						
4. Sings with group						
5. Experiments with rhythm instruments						
6. Creates art projects						
7. Constructs (paints, molds, etc.) recognizable figures						
Level V						
1. Participates in a wide variety of creative activities: finger plays, rhythm band, working with clay, painting, outdoor play, housekeeping, singing, etc.						

2.	Produces objects at the carpentry table; tells about them					
3.	Produces art objects: tells about them					
4.	Searches for better ways to construct					
5.	Builds complex block structures					
6.	"Plays" with new words					
7.	Evaluates his work (compares, describes, suggests improvement)					

G. CONCEPT DEVELOPMENT (Cause-effect, conserving, sorting, grouping, space, weight, time)

QUANTITATIVE Level III						
1.	Manipulates and experiments with simple machines					
2.	Counts by rote 1-5					
3.	Concept of "first" and "last"					
4.	Concept of ordinal numbers through "third"					
5.	Identifies pieces of money: penny, nickel, dime					
6.	Developing value concept of money					
7.	Concept of time: morning, noon, today, tomorrow					
8.	Helps to create extended projects (block, sand table, etc.)					
9.	Recognizes basic shapes					
10.	Forms creative designs with materials					

11. Asks questions to gain problem-solving information					
12. Uses construction material for multiple purposes					
Level IV					
1. Identifies pairs of familiar objects (shoes, socks, gloves, earrings)					
2. Uses ordinal concepts through fifth					
3. Demonstrates concept of number through 10					
4. Identifies penny, nickel, dime, quarter, dollar					
5. Compares distance (height, width) to an independent object (stick, etc.)					
6. Compares difference in dimension (taller, shorter, thinner, etc.)					
7. Compares volume in separate container Describes objects from different visual perspectives					
Level V					
1. Compares methods of filling a space					
2. Groups objects into sets of equal number					
3. Compares elements of unequal sets (more than, fewer than, etc.)					
4. Demonstrates one-to-one correspondence					
5. Counts to one hundred					
6. Identifies numerals 1 to 100 (book pages)					
7. Orders numbers 1 to 10					

8. Identifies number in group (mark five cars)					
9. Combines (adds) total number and two small groups					

H.   LANGUAGE

Level III					
1. Most language is intelligible					
2. Knows the name of the school					
3. Responds correctly to simple instructions involving locations					
4. Uses pronouns correctly					
5. Uses sentences of 4-5 words					
6. Recognizes and labels (verbally) 100-200 common objects					
7. Knows parents' names					
8. 1000+ word vocabulary					
Level IV					
1. Uses simple position words (over, under, etc.)					
2. Uses simple action words (run, walk, etc.)					
3. Uses complete sentences					
4. Uses personal pronouns					
5. Uses language for specific purposes: directions, information, etc.					
6. Repeats routine events					

Level V						
1. Communicates ideas, feelings, and emotions in well-formed sentences						
2. Uses correct form of most verbs in informal conversation						
3. Uses correct prepositions to denote place and position						
4. Uses most personal pronouns correctly						
5. Repeats nursery rhymes						
6. Sings with group and alone						
7. Explains operation of simple machines (pencil sharpener, etc.)						
8. Uses language to get what he wants						
9. Vocabulary of about 2000-4000 words						
(SOCIAL KNOWLEDGE)						
10. Can state full name						
11. Can state parents' full names						
12. Can state age						
13. Can state birthday						
14. Can state address						
15. Follows common directions						

I. READING READINESS

Level V: Auditory and Visual Discrimination						
1. Discriminates between similar sounds made by different objects						
2. Discriminates between initial phonemes: bat/cat, fat/rat, plat/flat, sat/hat, fan/Dan						
3. Discriminates between medial phonemes: bet/bit, bat/but, bit/bat, bin/ban						
4. Discriminates between final phonemes: bat/bar, can/car, bet/bed						
5. Follows moving object with eyes, side to side at reading distance						
6. Draws circles with closed ends						
7. Connects dots with straight pencil lines						
8. Follows left-to-right progression of pointer as adult reads						
9. Identifies letters of the alphabet						
10. Matches upper and lower case letters						
11. Identifies his first name in print						
12. Picks out like words and symbols on a printed page						
13. Identifies recurring words on experience chart						
COMPREHENSION SKILLS						
14. Listens to and follows verbal directions						
15. Locates elements in a picture (tallest, largest, etc.)						
16. Retells a story read to him in correct sequence						

17.	Answers recall questions about story characters, actions, etc.					
18.	Draws analogies from story to his own experience					
19.	Predicts and/or constructs story ending					
20.	Suggests titles for experience stories					
21.	Retells experiences in organized fashion					
22.	Reorganizes pictures to show correct story sequence					
23.	Makes value judgments about story events					

*Using an Anecdotal Record Form

Often we are presented with incomplete or insufficiently specific information on a child we have been assigned to teach. In such cases, one of our first responsibilities is to collect this information. A structured anecdotal record form is often helpful for recording the teacher's observations. Look at the form on the next page, reading the categories carefully. This form was actually used for collecting information on a child who had very little language skill. Since the teacher who designed this form had some previous knowledge about the child, she knew how to label parts of the form and knew the approximate amount of space to allow for jotting down words and phrases to record her observations.

Activity

Design an anecdotal record form (see page 39) that would be appropriate for gathering information on an exceptional child you know or have observed. Explain your format and categories. How will the information help you plan educational programs for the child?

Observations to Facilitate Program Planning

It is important to gather as much information as possible about a child before designing an educational program. If a child has been classified as handicapped, assessment data (information about present functioning levels in various developmental domains) are used to choose objectives, teaching methods and materials, and evaluation procedures for the Individualized Educational Program (IEP). Some assessment data are gathered by specialists such as school psychologists, but classroom teachers are also responsible for continual monitoring or evaluation. Much of the information that is important to classroom teachers is best gathered by direct observation of the child in the educational setting. The following activities will help you sharpen your observation skills and apply observational data to planning instruction.

For these activities you will need to observe (either on film or in real life) a child with a learning problem of some sort. You will complete two observation forms: One concerns choosing criterion measures (setting the standard to decide when a child has accomplished the objective) and the other concerns choosing appropriate teaching techniques.

*Form developed by Sara Willoughby-Herb. It appears in Individualized Education for Preschool Exceptional Children by J. T. Neisworth, S. Willoughby-Herb, S. Bagnato, C. Cartwright, and K. Laub, © 1980. Reprinted by permission of Aspen Systems Corp., Germantown, Md.

ANECDOTAL RECORD				
			_____ (child's name)	
			_____ (observer)	
			_____ (date)	
CHILD BEHAVIORS			TEACHER BEHAVIORS	
words said (or other specific behaviors)	words comprehended	words attempted	reinforcers used successfully	events being paired with reinforcement
general tasks enjoyed	specific behaviors at those tasks		vocabulary used	situation in which used

OTHER COMMENTS:

ANECDOTAL RECORD

Part 1: Choosing Appropriate Criterion Measures

Using a list of objectives already determined as appropriate for the child you are observing, watch the child performing the behaviors set forth in the objectives. Using the form on the next page, check the category that applies for each objective. You can get information about the objectives by asking the child's teacher or, if an IEP has been prepared for the child, reading the objectives on the IEP form.

Link your observation data to criterion statements for each objective using the following measures:

How the behavior was rated	Suggested criterion measure
1. absent or poorly developed	frequency, accuracy
2. inconsistent	frequency, rate, duration
3. occurs in restricted conditions	latency, frequency, rate
4. not in correct form	accuracy

Write out a specific criterion measure that you consider appropriate for each behavior you observed.

Part 2: Choosing Effective Teaching Techniques

In order to plan the best teaching strategies we must know how certain environmental events affect the child. We need to know how the child interacts with certain kinds of materials, behaves during certain activities or in areas of the classroom, or reacts to teacher instructions. Use the chart on page 42 to record your observations of these variables.

For each of the objectives and criterion statements you completed in Part 1, write out a statement of instructional methods and materials you consider appropriate, based on the information you've just collected.

Objectives	Absent or poorly developed	Incon- sistent	Occurs in restricted conditions	Not in correct form

	Lead to desirable behaviors	Lead to undesirable behaviors
Classroom settings		
Materials		
Activities		
Classroom prompts (reactions to verbal, visual cues, etc.)		

Assessing Program Characteristics

If we are to achieve a good match between the needs of children and ways they can be helped, we must have information about children and about program characteristics. Reynolds and Birch* designed a set of rating forms to be used in assessing program characteristics. The forms are reprinted on the following pages (see page 44). Each of the twelve forms is about a separate characteristic; the descriptive statements (five for each form) are arranged in order from 1 (least conducive to mainstreaming) to 5 (most conducive to mainstreaming).

Try one or more of the twelve forms by observing and rating in a classroom or special education program. If possible, do this as a group activity and compare your ratings with those of others in the group.

1. Which characteristics were the easiest to observe?

2. Which were the most difficult?

3. Which characteristics yielded the best agreement among raters?

4. Which yielded the poorest agreement?

5. Did you feel well qualified to do the ratings?

6. Did you observe aspects of the program that you considered relevant that are not included on the rating forms?

7. What is your general assessment of the worth of the forms for selecting appropriate programs for exceptional children?

*M. Reynolds, and J. Birch, Education for Exceptional Children in All America's Schools (Reston, Va.: Council for Exceptional Children, 1977), pp. 134-149.

Rating Sheet 1*
Space and Facility Accommodations to Physical Impairments

	1. (a) The classroom is essentially untreated for sound; (b) access to the class involves difficult elevation and entry problems for students in wheelchairs; (c) there are no amplification devices; (d) there are no partitioned areas for small group work; (e) movement to washrooms, lunch rooms, and other essential areas is difficult for the orthopedically or visually impaired students; (f) space is very limited—thus inflexible; and (g) storage space is almost totally lacking in classroom.
	2. At least four of the seven limitations (a through g above) are characteristic of the classroom spaces.
	3. General architectural accommodations (elevation changes) have been managed, but internal spaces are essentially untreated and inflexible.
	4. Basic architectural accommodations are adequate. Classroom and other spaces are generally adequate in size and sound treatment is adequate; but storage, furniture, and flexibility of space are significant problems.
	5. The classroom is carpeted and/or otherwise treated effectively for sound control; access and entry present no problems for any student; storage, flexible partitioning possibilities, sound amplification, varied furniture, and like matters are provided adequately.

*Source (for all rating sheets): M. Reynolds, and J. Birch, Education for Exceptional Children in All America's Schools. (Reston, Va.: Council for Exceptional Children, 1977), pp. 134-149. Reprinted by permission.

Rating Sheet 2
Teaching-Learning Settings

	1. Desks of uniform design are placed in neat rows and columns, all facing a teacher's desk.
	2. Desks of uniform design are placed in neat rows and columns, all facing in the same direction; at least one "special interest center" is added.
	3. Students sit in desks or at tables that are not in row by column arrangements and that interact with variously spaced interest centers.
	4. Instructional space is complex, involving a variety of learning centers and a variety of ways students can place themselves.
	5. Instructional space is divided into a variety of areas or learning centers that include room for both materials and students. Areas outside of the classroom, both within the school and in the larger community, are used with significant frequency and in organized ways.

Rating Sheet 3
Materials

	1. The instructional materials include essentially only one or at most three textbooks of standard grade level difficulty that are used with near uniformity by all students.
	2. Instructional materials include several levels (different reading levels) of basic textbooks covering content of the class. Additional materials from the library are on hand regularly for use by students.
	3. All the items in 2 are available, plus occasionally the teacher uses films, filmstrips, audio tapes, overhead projections, and similar audio-visual aids.
	4. All of the items in 2 and 3 exist plus permanent provision of a variety of materials in established interest centers for use in the teaching-learning of the class.
	5. Instructional materials include several levels of reading materials, plus collections of audiovisual materials, instructional games, and competency examinations. Students are able to "store" in the classroom their individual sets of materials and records. Students are competent in use of all equipment. Special instructional materials centers and consultants are available to assist teachers.

Rating Sheet 4
Classroom Management

1. Classroom management—including group alerts and communications, transitions, question and answer procedures—tend to be at least mildly chaotic and noisy. Only a minority of students tend to be thoroughly attentive or "on task" at most times.
2. Group signals and alerts are generally well attended, and at least half of students are "on task" at most times; but transition periods tend to be chaotic and behavior disturbances are handled unpredictably. Materials management and record keeping are at minimum acceptability levels.
3. Teacher-pupil and pupil-pupil communication and management are all in good order, but mainly on the basis of the high force level of the teacher. Teacher authority is clear. Predictability of class behavior is high because negative consequences for misbehavior are high—a tough but not highly competent situation.
4. Communication is good, organization is complex but orderly, attention level is high, and disturbance rate is low. The teacher is creative, adaptive, and shares responsibilities for the environment with students and rationalizes rules in group sessions. There are some bad days, but most are tolerable to good.
5. At least 90% of students attend when the teacher seeks to alert the full class; questions almost always serve as signals for all students; systems for transitions, record keeping, materials management, and like matters are well understood and observed efficiently. Students are clear about expectations and consequences of their behavior.

Rating Sheet 5
Social Environment

1.   Students are expected to work essentially alone as far as instructional tasks are concerned. Student-student relationships tend to be nonsharing, even competitive. The teacher rewards individual performance and seems nondeliberate about group processes.
2.   Students work mainly in isolation, but occasionally in small groups. The teacher praises and supports friendly interactions, but no systematic provision for education in group processes is provided. Evaluation tends to be individually oriented and to encourage competition.
3.   Students work in small groups frequently and must share materials. All records are individual. Students are expected to learn to work with each other, but goals are nonspecific.
4.   Students are clustered so that they can interact freely. Some group projects are assigned with considerable frequency. Group projects are evaluated informally, but grade records emphasize individual achievements. Social skills are valued.
5.   The development of positive social skills and attitudes is one avowed objective of the teacher. Students are expected to interact and share with each other and to help one another. Sometimes they work on group projects, dividing up work. The teacher assists in group process and rewards effective group work. Students have every reason to be mutually helpful. Definite efforts are made to provide socially integrative experiences for exceptional students.

Rating Sheet 6
Recognizing and Appreciating Cultural and Socioeconomic Differences

1. Instruction proceeds with little or no explicit recognition of cultural differences. The majority values and styles dominate the scene.
2. Special arrangements for remedial work are made for students who may have second language problems or who have different developmental patterns and learning styles associated with race or ethnicity. Teachers may have had required human relations training.
3. Special projects oriented to needs of minority students are arranged to supplement the regular school programs such as special preschool language classes, bilingual youth advocates, or special units on American Indian education or Black studies.
4. Efforts are made to go beyond special projects and to redesign the basic curriculum to include valid elements from all relevant cultures— so that all children can feel that both their past and their future are given studied and valued consideration.
5. Content, materials, and methods of instruction are made meaningful to minority group children, as well as to all others; the commitment to cultural pluralism is real, especially as reflected in curriculum. Both students and parents from minority communities feel engaged and well understood in the school situation; they feel as equals among equals. Aesthetic experiences of the school include samples from all cultures represented by the school.

Rating Sheet 7
Control of and Responsibility for Environment

	1. Each individual class and the school is a rule-governed operation, with rules based almost totally on the teacher's "police" power and competencies.
	2. Students share occasionally in discussion of how the school environment shall be managed. A degree of "consent of the governed" is achieved.
	3. Formal arrangements are made for the regular involvement of students in governance—as in student government, student management of classroom materials, weekly class meetings, or the like.
	4. Individual students and groups of students are given special training and responsibility for management of much of the school environment and processes. Included are technical matters such as running audio-visual machines, administering competency exams, orienting new students, and showing the school to visitors. In addition, training may be included in counseling skills (listening, reinforcing, etc.) and other aspects of interpersonal and group behavior.
	5. Students share significantly in the governance (policy making and administration) of their classes and school. Their obligations run to other students as well as to school officials; they are expected to help make the learning environment productive. They receive instruction, where necessary, to help them take responsibilities. The teacher shares in all of this as well, but gives particular attention to instruction for constructive initiatives and "autonomy" by students.

Rating Sheet 8
Content (Curriculum)

	1. Content is defined totally by the textbook or teachers' guide, including the sequence of topics of activities. The content and sequence are uniform for all students.
	2. The teacher basically follows a textbook or teachers' guide in setting content and sequence of topics, but introduces significant modifications or "special" topics, designed to accommodate the general interests of the group and the teacher's judgment of priorities. The program is almost totally uniform for all students.
	3. The teacher basically follows a textbook or curriculum guide but uses more than one level or set of textbooks in heterogeneous classes.
	4. Content for particular students is specified by the teacher; several levels of textbooks are used along with varieties of other instructional materials. Task sequences are carefully defined. Students are assessed individually and entered into instructions at appropriate levels.
	5. Student interests guide selection of a significant portion of the content. The program for each student is sequenced according to evaluation of previous performance and achievement. Attempts are made to integrate specific tasks across broader domains of the curriculum.

Rating Sheet 9
Degree of Structure

	1. Structure is attended to only casually. No systematic effort is made to control the degree of structure.
	2. Structure is imposed on some topics—those considered most essential; all students tend to receive similar treatment.
	3. All students receive a carefully structured approach in introducing concepts or new content. Students who complete work rapidly are free to proceed in their own way in their "extra" time.
	4. Instruction is varied in degree of structure, so that all students have a variety of experiences. Degree of structure tends to be a function of teacher interest and not fully a function of student need, but all students experience variety.
	5. Degree of structure is varied systematically so that students who need high structure get it and those who achieve better by creating their own structure are encouraged to do so. The teacher has structure clearly worked out for his/her teaching area and uses it creatively.

Rating Sheet 10
Instructional Methods

1. In a typical month, the teacher uses systematically no more than two of the methods listed.
2. In a typical month, the teacher uses systematically no more than three of the listed methods.
3. In a typical month, the teacher uses systematically at least five of the listed methods.
4. In a typical month, the teacher uses systematically at least five of the above methods and is studying or consulting with other school staff members about additional approaches for some students.
5. The teacher is able to use at least six of the above methods and has collaborative arrangements with special education teachers, school consultants, psychologists, or others to help implement additional methods as needed.

Rating Sheet 11
Rate of Learning

	1. All students are given fixed, uniform assignments to complete in uniform periods of time.
	2. All students are given uniform minimum assignments for standard periods of time. Students who complete work rapidly are usually free to work on *unrelated* activities. Students who do not complete work successfully continue with classmates in spite of poor background. Some extra help to "laggards" may be given.
	3. All students are given uniform minimum assignments for standard periods of time. Students who complete tasks rapidly and well are allowed informally to proceed to more advanced *related* topics. Students who fail to complete tasks satisfactorily are given extra tasks and/or assigned to others for extra help, such as aides or resource teachers.
	4. Students are given mastery examinations at *set times* such as at the beginning or end of each semester. After each evaluation, subgroups proceed at different rates and in different levels of the curriculum.
	5. Students proceed with instruction at rates indicated by mastery examinations. Such exams may be taken at any appropriate time, followed by pretests for succeeding tasks or topics. Entry to new areas may proceed at any time.

Rating Sheet 12
Evaluation

1. Evaluation is almost totally test oriented and always involves comparisons with other class members. Results are recorded as percentiles, percentages, standard scores, or some such metric, usually with no breakdown for diagnostic purposes. Scores are not interpreted in "mastery" terms. Atmosphere stresses grades and competition.
2. Evaluation is test oriented and norm oriented, but with careful attention to domain. Some modest degree of use is made of results in assigning "makeup" work or in other limited adjustments of the program.
3. Evaluation is mainly domain oriented and reasonably clear for domain. All exams are "handed back," but attention is mainly on "grading," rather than on the planning of instruction. Procedures tend to be somewhat inconsistent.
4. Most assessments are mastery oriented and clear about domain and are used effectively and regularly in planning instruction. Feedback to students on all tests is complete and clear. However, term grades tend to be assigned quite strictly on a norm or social comparison basis. Students are encouraged to evaluate their own work independently.
5. Assessments are partly test oriented, but include informal observations and assessments as well. All evaluation is clear as to domain and is mastery oriented. Assessments are quite frequent and integral parts of instruction. Occasionally norm oriented tests are used to give students a basis for comparison of their rates of development with that of others. All students have a solid chance for sensing progress. The teacher is aware that not all learning can be assessed by another person and that people must evaluate their own growth and what conditions for growth are optimal—as part of the total evaluation program.

Section B: Generic Teaching Skills

Having a Philosophy

Each of us has a viewpoint—whether we know it or not—on how human beings grow and develop. The purpose of this activity is to help you identify your viewpoint. A checklist, "Where Do You Stand on Development?" is given on the following pages. We adapted a more comprehensive checklist, "Where Do You Stand on Human Development?" which was published in 1972, by Educational Products Information Exchange Institute of New York, to arrive at our checklist.

1. Turn to the checklist on the following pages and complete it. Don't read any further until you have responded to the checklist.
-------------------------STOP—COMPLETE CHECKLIST-------------------------
Finished with the checklist? OK, then proceed.

2. Go back over your answers checking to see how many items you answered A, how many B, and how many C. Here's the key to interpreting your responses: If the majority of your answers are A, you are essentially an environmentalist. You believe that human development is shaped largely by events in the child's environment.

If the majority of your answers are B, you are essentially a maturationist. You believe that human development is shaped largely by what the child has inherited. You are a believer in "letting nature take its course."

If the majority of your answers are C, you take an interactionist view of development. You believe that there is a qualitative give-and-take between heredity and environment—that the child actively shapes and is shaped by the environment.

3. Decide which viewpoint is yours. Are you surprised? Are you something different than you would have originally thought? Make a list of ten teacher behaviors that would be consistent with your viewpoint. Check your list with a colleague. Does the colleague feel you have listed teacher behaviors that are logically related to your stand on human development? Modify your list if you need to.

4. Study the chart titled "Explanations of Development" on page 60, and the chart titled "Developmental Concepts Used in Educational Curriculums" on page 61. How does your list of teaching behaviors compare with the ideas presented in these charts? Do you need to make additional modifications in your list to ensure that it is consistent with your stand on human development?

5. Try the checklist out on your friends. Where do they stand on human development?

*Where Do You Stand on Development?

Answer the following questions by selecting the statements that best
describe your own beliefs about child development.

1. What is development? What is it that takes place in the individual?

A

☐ Development consists of pro-
gressive changes in behavior
as the individual is shaped
by his/her environment.

☐ Developmental behavior
changes become increasingly
complex. The simpler pat-
terns are the prerequisites
for higher level or more
complex patterns.

B

☐ Development is the unfolding
or maturation of genetically
programmed patterns of behavior.

☐ Development is the growth or
formation of internal structures that form the basis of
specific behaviors or skills.

C

☐ Development consists of pro-
gressive changes in internal
structures and behaviors
that are the combined re-
sults of biological growth
and learning.

2. What is the course of development?

A

☐ Development takes place continuously. Each new skill or
behavior is added to the individual's behavior pattern.
The difference between a
younger and an older person
is the amount of time each
has had to learn.

B

☐ Development progresses in
stages that are biologically
determined. Each stage must
be fully completed before one
is ready to progress to the
next.

C

☐ Development progresses
through stages determined
by the individual's matur-
ity and learning.

*Adapted from "Where Do You Stand on Human Development," EPIE Report No. 42. Available from Educational
Products Information Exchange Institute, P.O. Box 620, Stony Brook, NY 11790. Reprinted by permission.

3. When does development take place? When is the individual ready to learn?

A

☐ Development occurs only when the individual has mastered or been taught the prerequisite skills or behaviors.

B

☐ Development occurs only when the individual is biologically or maturationally ready.

C

☐ Learning will take place when the individual has mastered the basic skills, but will be easier and more efficient if the individual is also "mature" enough to sustain the learning.

4. What sets the limits or hampers development?

A

☐ Learning or development will continue indefinitely as long as the environment provides the necessary incentives and opportunities for learning.

B

☐ An individual will reach his/her genetically determined potential unless blocked by traumatic circumstances in the environment.

C

☐ Development will continue within the limitation set by the individual's environment and heredity.

Go back to page 56 and proceed with an analysis of your responses.

Explanations of Development

	Environment (nurture)	Interaction	Heredity (nature)
Source:	Learning from the environment	Learning and maturation	Maturation of genetic potential
Important Area of Study:	Environmental variables	Environmental and person variables	Person variables
Developmental Concepts:	1. Individual differences are the result of unique learning histories.	1. Individual differences are the result of the combined effects of genetic and environmental differences.	1. Individual differences are the result of genetically determined biological differences.
	2. The individual is shaped by the external environment.	2. The individual is the combined product of his/her unique biological makeup and environment. He/she is shaped, and in turn, shapes his/her environment.	2. The individual is an adaptive organism, genetically programmed as a result of the process of evolution.
	3. An individual's potential is unlimited.	3. The individual's potential is determined by environmental and hereditary factors.	3. Developmental potential is "fixed" at conception.
Pattern of Development:	Continuous and cumulative	Additive within stages	Biological stages
Developmental Readiness:	Development takes place when the individual has learned the prerequisite skills and behaviors.	Both maturational and learning levels determine readiness to progress developmentally. The prerequisites of each completed stage facilitate learning.	Developmental progress to the next biological stage is genetically controlled. Premature training will have detrimental effects.

Developmental Concepts Used in Educational Curriculums

Rationale: People's implicit theories or views of development influence their selection of curricular designs and their beliefs in what and how their children should be taught.

Concepts of
Development: Development occurs in stages.

                   Development occurs continuously.

Examples of
Curriculums: Normative sequencing (based on age norms)

                   Hierarchical sequencing (based on pro-
                   gressive difficulty)

                   Age: 30-35 months

Can indicate where fingers, shoes, etc.   Indicates objects named in response to
are (30 months)   "Where is _____?"

Identifies pictures from name (seven out   Names objects in response to "What is
of ten) (30 months)   this?"

Understands concept of 1 (30 months)   Points to pictured objects in response
                                               to "Where is _____?"
Says ten words in a group (30.5 months)

Matches blocks of four colors   Names a pictured object.
(30.8 months)   Points to self when asked "Who's
                                               _____?"
Gives first and last name (32 months)

Repeats two digits (33 months)   Gives first name when asked "What is
                                               your name?"
Can point to teeth, chin, on request   Gives full name when asked "What is
(34 months)   your name?"

Rewarding Children's Appropriate Behavior

Good teachers seem to reward children automatically for behaving appropriately and to ignore their occasional inappropriate behaviors. Observe a good teacher during a small- or large-group instructional activity, recording how often he or she rewards appropriate behaviors and ignores inappropriate ones. Use the chart on the next page to record your observation.

Discussion

Compare your findings with those of your colleagues. What seems to be the average rate of reinforcement— (number of reinforcements/time observed)—delivered by these teachers? Do the reinforcement rates vary across age groupings (preschool, primary grades, etc.)?

Optional

If you have an opportunity to work with children, collect data on your own reinforcement rate for 5 minutes. Do this for four or five days. How do you compare with the "good" teachers you and your classmates observed?

Using Prompts to Facilitate Learning

Children find many tasks difficult at first, unless we provide them with some assistance (a prompt). Prompts may be verbal, visual, or manual. For example, in teaching Billy to make a capital B, we could prompt him by:

> *Saying, "Make a top-bottom line with two bumps"—verbal prompt
> *Making a worksheet with dotted B's for tracing—visual prompt
> *Guiding his hand as he writes—manual prompt

Whatever prompt (or prompts) teachers choose, it is important to remember that the eventual goal is for the children to perform the tasks without the use of prompts. Therefore, we must fade or gradually reduce the prompts we use. We can fade prompts by making them less intense (making the dotted lines for the B less and less dark), less frequent (making fewer dots for the child to trace), etc.

Date _____

Lesson content _____

Minutes observed _____

    frequency, reinforced appropriate behaviors _____

_____

_____

    frequency, reinforced <u>inappropriate</u> behaviors _____

_____

_____

    frequency, ignored <u>inappropriate</u> behaviors _____

_____

_____

<u>General Comments</u>:

1. What kinds of rewards did the teacher use?

2. What did you classify as appropriate behaviors? inappropriate behaviors?

3. (Other)

Rules for Prompting

There are two rules to remember in using prompts well:

1.   Choose a prompt that can be easily faded.
In the following illustration, the teacher is using a manual prompt to assist the student in walking up the stairs. In the scene on the left, the manual prompt also includes a visual prompt (child sees teacher helping her). This visual prompt cannot be faded gradually—the teacher is either in front of the child or not.

Incorrect   Correct

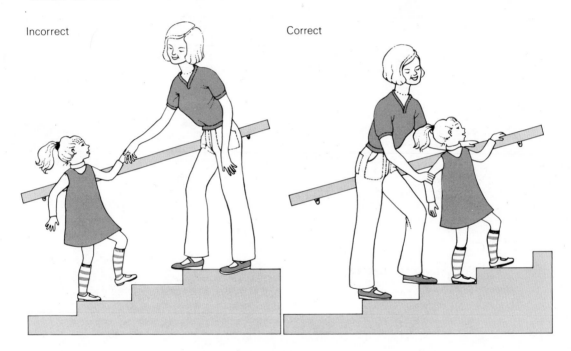

2.   Choose a prompt that focuses on some significant characteristics of the task.
Prompts should facilitate learning the task, not merely completion of it.
In the illustration on p. 65, a picture of a bee is used to prompt the child to recall the letter name. The prompt in each illustration will facilitate the child's naming of the letter. However, the prompt in the second picture is printed over a significant aspect of the letter B—the two bumps. The child taught by this prompt will learn to look at that part of the letter. This should facilitate learning what the letter B looks like.

Incorrect

Correct

Design Your Own Prompts

Share your ideas with your colleagues if possible.

1. You are teaching finger spelling to a hearing handicapped child. She has difficulty differentiating between the letters U and V. She uses the U sign for both letters. How would you use prompting to teach her how to spell V correctly? Assume that you must use visual and/or manual prompts. Plan how you would fade your prompts as well. Record your plans below.

U   V

_____

_____

_____

_____

_____

_____

_____

_____

_____

_____

2.   Mary is a physically handicapped child; she has mild cerebral palsy. She has some control of her arms, and her teachers are attempting to teach her to write. Their first objectives are to teach her to make straight vertical and horizontal lines. Describe a prompting procedure you might use to teach these objectives. Remember Mary's disability—she will have jerky movements and will find it difficult to control her movements.

_____

_____

_____

_____

_____

_____

_____

_____

_____

_____

_____

Using Reinforcement Appropriately

Behavioral psychologists have demonstrated the importance of reinforcement in learning. Stated simply, <u>reinforcement occurs whenever an event immediately following a behavior causes that behavior to increase in frequency</u>. We know that reinforcement works when used immediately and consistently.

Using reinforcement well in the classroom is not simply giving children sweets or praise after each desirable behavior. A teacher who uses reinforcement appropriately considers:

> *<u>Type</u> of reinforcement most appropriate for individual children
> *Appropriate <u>amount</u> of reinforcement
> *Ways to aim children constantly toward more mature types and levels of reinforcement

In the next exercises you will be involved in these considerations as you plan reinforcement techniques.

Selecting the Appropriate Reinforcer

1. You are given a reinforcer hierarchy below. The reinforcers at the beginning of the hierarchy (particularly the first three) are the most unnatural and contrived; those at the end are most mature and natural. Read the items in the hierarchy and be certain that you understand the categories.

Reinforcer Hierarchy

a. Primary, e.g., food
b. Tangible, e.g., little toys
c. Tangible and Generalized, e.g., tokens
d. Task-imbedded, e.g., teacher makes a game out of memorizing multiplication tables
e. Activity, e.g., teacher gives children a play period after a difficult task
f. Social, e.g., child receives attention from teacher, peers, etc.
g. Informational Feedback, e.g., child gets information concerning correctness of tasks in a variety of ways—programmed texts, graded assignments
h. Intrinsic, child seems to be providing own motivation, e.g., child enjoys subject matter or finds achievement itself rewarding

Observe at least two children in a teaching-learning setting. Record the frequency and types of reinforcers that seem to be maintaining the children's behaviors. Make a summary statement concerning where each child seems to be operating within this hierarchy. Do you think these types of rewards are developmentally appropriate?

Record your summary statements here.

_____

_____

_____

_____

_____

_____

Selecting the Appropriate Amount of Reinforcement

2.   Teachers must be concerned about delivering the appropriate <u>amount</u> as well as type of reinforcement. Within any one classroom, children's reinforcement needs vary widely.

Observe a teacher during small-group instruction. Record the <u>frequency</u> of reinforcement given to each child within the group.

children's
names →

number of times teacher rewards
in _____ minutes

What differences do you see within this group in terms of amount of reinforcement delivered by the teacher? Why do you think these differences exist? Do you think the teacher's reinforcement rates are appropriate? Jot down your responses here.

_____

_____

_____

_____

_____

_____

_____

_____

_____

Aiming Toward Most Appropriate Reinforcement Levels

3. Observe a child who has some noticeable developmental delays. Determine (a) the type and amount of reinforcement that currently maintains that child's behavior, and (b) the type and amount of reinforcement that would be most normal and developmentally appropriate for that child.

To determine the most normal reinforcement type and amount, find, through observation, the norm for nondelayed children of that same age. What are your findings? Report them here.

_____

_____

_____

_____

_____

_____

_____

To help determine the most developmentally appropriate type and amount of re-inforcement for this child, read what developmentalists say about the devel-opment of motivational systems (e.g., compare Lawrence Kohlberg's Levels of Moral Development to the reinforcement hierarchy). Where would you expect a child of this age to be functioning in terms of motivation?

_____

_____

_____

_____

_____

_____

_____

_____

_____

Planning Varied and Immediate Reinforcers

4.   When children are working independently or in open settings, it is often challenging for teachers to deliver immediate reinforcement. Here are techniques developed by some teachers:

   a.   Alice needed some immediate reward for using the "s" sound correctly. Her teacher taped a tally card on Alice's desk. Alice kept tally each time she used "s" correctly. The tally card reminded Alice to use the "s" sound, and reminded her teacher to reward her efforts.

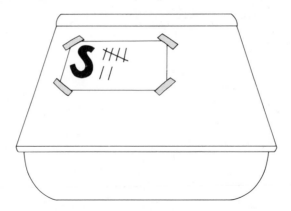

   b.   To make practicing computation more fun, a teacher covered the answers with peel-off stickers. The children worked the problems, wrote their answers, and peeled off the stickers to check their answers. This technique could be used for any kind of practice work, such as English, social studies.

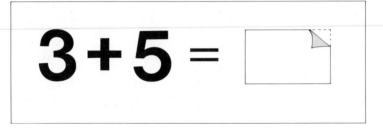

c. A nursery school child almost never remembered to put toys away as she went from center to center. And the staff often forgot to remind and reward her for picking up. The head teacher gave the child a chart to wear. Each time the child picked up toys, the head teacher or a staff member put a star on the child's chart. As in the first example, the chart was a good reminder for both staff and child, as well as an immediate reward.

Choose three other situations in which a child might need immediate reinforcement, and design delivery methods. Share your ideas with your colleagues if possible, evaluating the originality and practicality of each. You might want to record some of your colleagues' suggestions for future reference.

Using Differential Reinforcement

Teachers who want to use reinforcement well must first master the skill of using differential reinforcement, that is, delivering a high frequency of reinforcers for a particular (desired) behavior while ignoring other (undesired) behaviors.

Try the following role-play situations to see how well you can use differential reinforcement. You will need at least three people for each role-play situation: a teacher, a child, and an observer. The observer will record how well the teacher differentially rewards the student. Use the recording sheet on the next page.

```
┌─────────────────────────────────────────────────────────────────────┐
│                        Observation Record                            │
└─────────────────────────────────────────────────────────────────────┘
```

length of observation _____ teacher _____

1. no. times teacher reinforced appropriate behavior _____

2. no. times child performs appropriate behavior _____

3. no. times teacher reinforced <u>inappropriate</u> behavior _____

4. no. times child performs inappropriate behavior _____

_____

Role-Play Situation 1

Mara is a preschooler who still sucks her thumb. Her teacher has decided to use differential reinforcement to discourage thumb-sucking. She will be very reinforcing to Mara at all times <u>except</u> when Mara's thumb is in her mouth. During thumb-sucking she will ignore Mara.

In this role-play, the teacher should read a book to Mara, remembering to use the differential reinforcement procedure described above. Mara will listen as any normal preschooler, but will occasionally suck her thumb. The observer will fill out all items on the recording sheet, except number 2.

Role-Play Situation 2

Jeffrey is a fourth grader who is not very attentive during lessons. His teacher wants to use differential reinforcement. Each time Jeffrey looks attentively at the teacher, at his work, complies with instructions, etc., his teacher will reward him. The teacher will ignore Jeffrey's inattentive-ness.

In this role-play, the teacher will teach Jeffrey how to complete the following multiplication matrices. The teacher will do part of the first one with Jeffrey, telling him what to do and where to write his answers. Jeffrey will be asked to complete that matrix and do the second one on his own. To be sure that Jeffrey has ample opportunity to follow directions, the teacher should use many directions, such as watch me, show me where I should write the answer, which number do I do next? Jeffrey will attend only randomly to the teacher. The observer will complete all items on the recording sheet, except number four. A pen or pencil of a different color can be used to distinguish observations for this role play from the first situation.

Matrices

X	2	4	6	8
2				
4				
6				
8				

X	3	4	5	6
3				
4				
5				
6				

Evaluation

After each group member has had an opportunity to play all three roles, discuss your experiences. Some questions you might address are:

1. Were the teachers pleased with their rates of reinforcement relative to the children's behavior?

2. How easily could the teachers maintain their differential reinforcement procedures while carrying on their teaching or reading tasks?

3. Could the students detect that differential reinforcement was being used?

4. What difficulties did the observers encounter?

5. How might teachers improve and monitor their skills in using differential reinforcement?

Using a Contingency Contract

Teachers often use contingency contracts to manage an individual student's problem, academic or behavioral. A contingency contract comprises a certain sequence of steps.

Events Comprising a Contingency Contract

1. Determine behavior and direction of change. (What behavior will you work on? Do you want it to increase or decrease?)

2. Determine consequence and relation to behavior. (What reward will be used? How much of the behavior is needed to earn the reward?)

3. Write up agreement.

4.   Child performs behavior.

5.   Assess adequacy of behavior. (Did the performance meet the standards set up in 2?)

6.   Deliver consequence.

Try using a contract with a friend, family member, or peer. Record the specifics of your contract and evaluate its effectiveness.

_____

_____

_____

_____

_____

_____

_____

_____

Suggestions for Contracts

_____

_____

_____

_____

_____

_____

_____

_____

Getting Rid of Undesirable Behaviors

All of us have experienced the phenomenon of forgetting. We seem to forget especially skills and information that we have no opportunity to use. For example, we forget an old friend's phone number or how to make the folded paper objects we learned to make in grade school.

We can "engineer" forgetting in order to help children get rid of undesirable behaviors; we do this by setting up situations in which children will have <u>no</u> opportunity to practice that behavior. For example, Billy, a six-year-old, ate paste every chance he got. The teacher put all paste jars out of reach. When pasting projects were being done, she saw to it that she was near Billy at all times. If his hand began to go near his mouth, she redirected it. She also praised Billy for not eating paste. Gradually, she could move further from Billy and allow him to use paste while unsupervised.

Structure an engineered forgetting procedure for these problems:

1. Preschoolers who ride tricycles all over the play yard

2. Grade schooler who <u>always</u> talks to neighbors during silent reading period

3. High school student who lingers when excused for errands

Using Shaping

Often we are faced with teaching new, difficult behaviors to children. We cannot simply ask a two-year-old to throw a ball across the room and expect him or her to do it. The child will, at first, have difficulty aiming the ball in the correct direction and/or throwing the ball such a great distance. We cannot <u>wait</u> for the child to accomplish that task (the terminal objective). We must shape—reinforce—small approximations toward the task. For example, we first reward the child for simply throwing the ball. After the child becomes proficient at this first approximation of the task, we withhold reinforcement until he or she makes a closer approximation. So, we might tell this child, "Good, but now throw it to <u>me</u>." Now we only reinforce throws that come <u>toward</u> us. After each successful step, we withhold reward until the child makes a closer approximation to the target.

In shaping, <u>the teacher cannot always predetermine the steps in the shaping process, but must watch the child closely and reinforce even slight approximations of the terminal objectives.</u> Some typical shaping sequences are:

1. The <u>terminal objective</u> is: Child repeats proper sentence when teacher says, "Mary, say this: 'Give me the pencil.'" The child's typical responses during shaping might be:

    a.   "pencil"
    b.   "give pencil"
    c.   "give me pencil"
    d.   "give me the pencil"

2.   The terminal objective is that the child will walk across the balance beam without falling. The child's typical responses during shaping are:

    a.   he or she takes two steps and is allowed down
    b.   he or she gradually increases number of steps until can walk all the way across

3.   Select a teaching objective and state <u>possible</u> steps toward approximation of that objective.

_____

_____

_____

_____

_____

_____

_____

_____

_____

_____

4.   Try out a shaping procedure with a friend. Select some action you would like your friend to perform. Reward approximations by clapping. Remember these two hints as you shape up your friend:

    a.   Be sure your friend is <u>consistently</u> performing one level of the behavior <u>before</u> you withhold reinforcement to wait for a closer approximation.
    b.   You might reward your friend for getting into a position (e.g., sitting, standing) that will facilitate performing the behavior you've chosen.

Record the results of your shaping on the next page.

_____

_____

_____

_____

_____

_____

_____

_____

_____

_____

_____

_____

Evaluating Contingency Management Systems

Contingency management systems (e.g., token economies, contract systems) are used by many special educators. Such systems can be quite rewarding for teachers—children may work quietly, cooperatively, and so on. However, we also want to be certain that such systems are most beneficial to the children, so special educators should periodically evaluate their management techniques.

Observe a classroom in which a specific management is used. (You might use one of the films from the resources section if a real life observation is impossible.) Use the following guidelines and then summarize your observations on p. 78, along with suggestions for improvement.

Guidelines for Evaluating Management Techniques

1. Does the technique result in the development of a normalized behavior?

2. Does the technique employ strategies that are normalized?

3. Does the technique enable the child to be educated with normal children to the maximum extent possible?

4. Does the technique directly relate to the objectives specified for the child?

5. Can we assess the effectiveness of the technique?

6. Does the technique lead to quick, efficient behavior changes?

7. Can the technique be applied to a range of behaviors?

8. Does the technique effectively reduce deviant behaviors?

9. Does the technique lead to independence?

10. Does the technique broaden the child's repertoire of effective positive and negative consequences in a way that will lead to more mature development?

11. Does the technique lead to desirable generalizations?

Summary and Suggestions

_____

_____

_____

_____

_____

_____

_____

_____

_____

_____

_____

_____

_____

_____

Checklist of General Teaching Skills

Before completing this section on generic teaching skills, you might want to
fill out this checklist, which has been used to evaluate student teachers.
The first section of the checklist refers to general behaviors of the student
teachers as members of the teaching staff. The second section refers to specific teaching skills used while directly teaching children. Record how you
perceive your own teaching behaviors, using a 1 to 5 rating, where 1 is low
and 5 is high. You might ask a peer or teacher to rate you as well, noting any
discrepancies. When you are finished, note areas in which you need to develop
skills; consider how you might do that.

<u>General Classroom Behaviors</u>
Rating 1 (low)-5 (high)

1. Is prepared for lessons upon arrival at school.

2. During open activities (e.g., before lunch, recess, early
    morning) is observant of needs of the whole group and goes
    to unsupervised areas, engaging children in activities.

3. Teaches <u>all</u> children to follow general classroom rules—
    such as, put away toys neatly and correctly when activi-
    ties change, look at books quietly before lunch.

4. Generally initiates activities and takes on responsibili-
    ties.

5. Attempts to be a positive reinforcer to the children in
    the classroom.

6. Is friendly and cooperative with other staff members.

7. Performs own cleaning responsibilities each day.

8. Communicates with parents in a positive manner.

Specific Teaching Behaviors

1. Plans lessons using developmentally appropriate objectives.

2. Plans appropriate strategies for teaching lessons (uses shaping, prompting, etc., when necessary).

3. Plans varied reinforcers.

4. Plans task-imbedded reinforcers.

5. Carries out teaching plan during instruction.

6. Can improvise if time remains after lesson is over.

7. Differentially reinforces appropriate behaviors during lessons.

8. Disciplines in a matter-of-fact manner.

9. Refrains from rewarding (through nagging, attention, etc.) inappropriate behaviors.

10. Can identify clearly which behaviors in children are appropriate and inappropriate.

11. Delivers large amounts of reinforcement to children who have problems, but only at appropriate instances.

12. Can substitute activities when plans appear inappropriate.

13. Is positive with the children.

14. Is enthusiastic during lessons.

15. Provides opportunities for each child to be successful at each lesson.

16. Shows creativity (diversity, fluency) in planning activities.

17. Imposes a minimum of "don'ts" upon children.

18. Moves from one objective to another before children complain or become tired.

19. Keeps children enthusiastic throughout lesson.

Section C: Curricular Adjustments

Planning Written Language Activities

In mainstreamed classrooms, we often find children whose written language skills fall far below the norm. It is important, however, for teachers to plan some language activities in which all children can participate equally. For example, after a field trip, it might be desirable to have all the children make and write similar thank-you messages. Some teachers have planned written language activities using words that are cut out of magazines and assembled to form the text or message; others have planned activities using pictures in place of words, and so on. Also, activities that do not require a lot of writing are good for total group participation—for example, making posters, bumper stickers.

Plan a written language activity that an entire fifth-grade class can participate in, even though three children have written language skills at the second-grade level. List your objectives and activities, telling why they are appropriate for everyone in the class.

Language Experience: Matching Developmental Level and Teaching Strategy

Teachers in the preschool and early grades often encounter youngsters with language delays. Many of these children need to develop more extensive vocabularies, listening skills, imitative skills, and so on. If we want to match our teaching techniques to the child's level of language development, merely providing drill experiences is not enough. A teacher using a developmental perspective will:

1. Identify the child's level of functioning according to normal developmental sequences (e.g., year 2, 3)

2. Identify language experiences that are effective for children at that developmental level

3. Plan teaching strategies that incorporate those normative language experiences

Assume you are a kindergarten teacher and have a child in your classroom who has the language characteristics described on p. 82. Follow the sequence of teacher tasks listed above and develop an educational prescription for that child.

Student description—Language skills

Names common objects when asked
Uses one-word requests
Responds to simple, clear requests from others
Does not use language for continued conversation with peers or adults
Uses mostly nouns and verbs
Answers first and last name

Planning Science Activities for Visually Handicapped Children

Science is an important aspect of any cognitively oriented curriculum. Through science activities children learn concepts, relationships, observational skills, analytic skills, skills in following directions, and so on. Since most science programs rely a great deal on visual participation, we have to adapt such programs if we wish to integrate visually handicapped students. Some ways to adapt instruction are:

1. Provide maximum tactile experiences.

2. Use clear auditory descriptions and explanations.

3. Emphasize taste and smell experiences where possible.

4. Keep the visually impaired child as active as the others so he or she does not become bored.

Choose a science unit from a popular kit or program. Study the objectives and activities. Describe, specifically, how you can adapt those activities for a child who is visually impaired. Are there any activities or objectives in which the child cannot participate?

Teaching Children to Listen

Auditory discrimination problems are common among many kinds of handicapping conditions—learning disabilities, speech and language problems, mental retardation, and so on. It is important, then, for teachers to integrate listening skills into the curriculum. Identify several interesting activities you could use to teach the following listening skills. Identify activities appropriate to preschool, primary, and intermediate levels.

1. Child recognizes source of sound.

2. Child recognizes sounds that are the same and sounds that are different.

3. Child labels distinct sounds.

4. Child labels similar sounds.

Increasing Vocabulary

Children with speech and language problems need to be exposed to good language models. Language experts suggest that we can increase a child's vocabulary by providing repeated examples of new vocabulary. Many children's stories, rhymes, and songs provide such repeated models. For example, in the following rhyme, children learn the words giant and elf and also learn the concepts "tall" and "small."

Tall and Small

Here is a giant who is tall, tall, tall;
    (Children stand up tall.)
Here is an elf who is small, small, small;
    (Children slowly sink to floor.)
The elf who is small will try, try, try
    (Children slowly rise.)
To reach to the giant who is high, high, high.
    (Children stand tall, stretch, and reach arms
    high.)

(Author Unknown)

Identify several rhymes, stories, and so on, at the preschool, primary, and intermediate level interest ranges that provide repeated experiences with words and hence can be used to expand children's vocabulary. A good resource is Rhymes for Fingers and Flannelboards by Louise B. Scott and J. J. Thompson, published by the Webster Division of McGraw-Hill in 1960.

Designing a Conversation Board

Many children with orthopedic handicaps have a concurrent communication problem. They hear, understand, and wish to communicate, but are physically unable to form the sounds needed for speech. However, these children can communicate with language boards. These boards are attached to trays and can be changed for different activities through the day. Words (nouns, verbs, adjectives, etc.) necessary for communication are printed on the boards and the child merely points in order to communicate.

For young children who do not yet read, conversation boards can be designed with pictorial symbols. A standardized system of this sort has also been developed (e.g., ♥↑ = happy; ♥↓ = sad).*

What kinds of words or symbols do you think a child would need to get along in a regular classroom? Design a conversation board that will serve a child's general needs (not subject-related) through the school day. Choose a general grade level. When you have finished, share your ideas with colleagues.

Developing a Guide for Educational Adjustments

Form study groups of four or five people if possible. Each group member is to do reading on the nature of one or two handicapping conditions, paying special attention to how teachers must adjust their instructional techniques in order to integrate children with those characteristics into a regular classroom. When all group members have done their research, prepare a master chart that can be used by a classroom teacher involved in mainstreaming.

Suggestions:

You may need to refer to introductory special education texts in determining the specific handicapping conditions you will study. Be certain that your list exhausts the types of exceptionalities encountered in mainstream education. Prepare a second list of (educational) variables that you will use in determining the types of adjustments necessary. In this second list, be certain to consider these aspects of educational programming: materials, instructional techniques, nature of behaviors required in instructional objectives. A sample of a possible master chart follows:

*Bliss Symbols. See G. C. Vanderheiden, and D. H. Harris-Vanderheiden, "Communication Techniques and Aids for the Nonvocal Severely Handicapped," in Communication Assessment and Intervention Strategies, ed. L. L. Lloyd (Baltimore: University Park Press, 1976), pp. 607-652.

	Areas of instructional adjustment		
Handicapping condition	Materials	Instructional methods	Student behavior for instructional objectives*
Hearing impairment	Use materials that focus on visual aspects of content.	Seat students so that speaker(s) may be seen at all times. Supplement with visual techniques as much as possible.	Students who have communication problems may not be asked to respond in a verbal mode, at times.
	etc.	etc.	etc.

*Here, you may wish, instead, to consider separate content areas in the elementary curriculum, such as math, reading, physical education.

Adjusting Instructional Objectives to Meet the Needs of Special Learners

Teachers who work in mainstreamed classes often find that they need merely to adjust certain aspects of their regular instructional objectives in order to integrate the special learners into large-group instructional activities. They might adjust any of the three characteristics required of an instructional objective: the behavior required of the learner, the conditions under which he or she is to perform, the minimum acceptable criterion.

Example:

Marian is a ten-year-old who spends approximately one hour a day mainstreamed in a regular fifth-grade classroom. Marian is a very large child, nearly non-verbal, and functions at a low level. She was most recently enrolled in a class for trainable retarded children. Her general performances in the functional domains follow:

Language: understands and follows simple directions; doesn't answer in class at all—just smiles; likes music—doesn't sing; talks to mother or teacher at home

Cognitive: low first-grade level, yet knows names of baseball teams, emblems, songs, football players

Social-Emotional: associates with adults more than with children; dependent at home

Motor: slow, clumsy, inactive, overweight

During part of the time that Marian is in the fifth-grade classroom, children are assigned to independent reading activities. During one of these activity periods the children were to follow this instructional objective:

After reading a short story independently, children will tell about their favorite character. Each child will identify that character by name and will state at least one reason for liking him/her.

The teacher was able to adjust that objective for Marian so that she could participate in the same general activity.

Adjusted objective: After listening to a story, Marian will identify her favorite character by pointing to his/her picture and by imitating the teacher's naming of the character.

Rationale for changes: The original objective required verbal and reading skills beyond Marian's abilities.

Objective components adjusted:
Behavior—points to picture
Conditions—after listening to a story
Criteria—has only to point and imitate name

Assignment

Read the learner descriptions below.

1. A preschooler—David is being mainstreamed in a preschool class for three- and four-year-olds. David has a limited social and language repertoire. In addition, he engages in some autistic-like behaviors. David's typical performances in the four functional domains are:

Language: David uses one-word utterances; these typically are imitative in nature and not used for self-expression. David appears to understand and follow most clear, simple directions, however.

Cognitive: David recognizes colors, numbers, and so on (most concepts that normal preschoolers recognize). Because of his language involvement, however, he does not verbalize these concepts. That is, he can, for example, find a red crayon; but he will not label it "red" when requested.

Social-Emotional: David seldom engages independently in cooperative or parallel play with other children. He appears to watch others playing, however. He has tantrums when frustrated—approximately three times a day. He is beginning to express affection by pats and kisses. David's attention span during lessons ranges from five to ten minutes.

Motor: David can engage in most motor tasks appropriate to a child of his age. His movements, however, are slow and stilted.

2.   An elementary-aged child—Mary is ten-years-old. She is now mainstreamed after having spent the past four years in a class for educable mentally retarded children. Mary's parents speak Spanish, and she is bilingual. Her performances in the four functional domains are:

Language: Mary has difficulty speaking and understanding English although when the speaker slows down, her comprehension improves. Mary's speech is very slow, so that a listener easily becomes bored and disinterested.

Cognitive: Mary is at grade level (fifth grade) in reading and spelling. She enjoys these. She is two years behind in math, however. She doesn't recall basic math facts quickly, calculates slowly even on paper, and has difficulty with word problems.

Social-Emotional: Mary is given many responsibilities at home—she often must care for an infant sister until late evening. She is more dependent on teacher support and attention than the other fifth graders, however. She prefers talking to the teacher to interacting with peers.

Motor: Mary's motor behaviors are all delayed in terms of rate. She is extremely slow and cautious in all movements. She does not enjoy activities, needless to say.

3.   A secondary-aged child, Peter is sixteen-years-old and attends a senior high school, where he spends a third of his day in a special class for trainable children, a third in a sheltered workshop, and a third integrated (e.g., for physical education, lunch, homeroom). Peter has serious problems controlling his aggressive, impulsive, and anger behaviors. His performances in the four functional domains are:

Language: Peter's language skills approximate normal development, although he often uses "vulgar" expressions in inappropriate situations (e.g., loudly, in the school cafeteria). He enjoys acquiring a sophisticated vocabulary.

Cognitive: Peter can read (that is, pronounce words) almost at grade level. However, his impulsivity hinders his comprehension. He generally cannot retell what he has read or answer questions regarding content. His math and spelling skills are at approximately third-grade level.

Social-Emotional: This is Peter's weakest area. He does not socialize well with his peers. However, he is meek around persons stronger than he! Otherwise, he is quick to hit, name-call, destroy, and so on. He does not attend well in class or obey his teachers, other than the special class teachers.

Motor: Peter's motor skills are adequate except in cases where his impulsiveness interferes. He is quite strong.

Choose an educational level within which to work. If you choose preschool, assume you have a mainstreamed class of three- and four-year-olds and you are working with David. If you choose elementary, assume you have a mainstreamed fifth grade and you are working with Mary. If you choose secondary, assume you have a mainstreamed sophomore homeroom and you are working with Peter.

If you have difficulty constructing objectives, refer to a normed list of developmental behaviors such as the one used in the Assessment section or refer to a published curriculum.

Using the form on the next page, write a behavioral objective, appropriate for normal learners, from each of the following curriculum areas: reading/language arts, social studies, science. Next, rewrite each objective, making it appropriate to the handicapped child described for your level. Identify the rationale for rewriting the objective. Identify the components of the objective (behavior, conditions, criterion) that were modified for the handicapped person.

Task Analysis

Task analysis skills are essential to good teaching. They are especially critical for special educators who often need to break down tasks so that specific skills involved can be identified and taught. In addition, task analysis allows us to pinpoint the specific task components with which children need extra assistance.

Task analysis is often a difficult skill for beginning teachers to acquire since they have little experience in teaching and watching children learn difficult tasks. One way to do a task analysis is for the teacher to perform the task or watch someone else perform it and to write down each step as it occurs as accurately as possible. Another way is to analyze tasks into behavior domains, asking questions such as what motor, verbal, auditory, conceptual/discrimination skills are involved.

Objective	Adjusted objectives	Adjustment rationale	Components adjusted

Example

This task analysis is used regularly by a kindergarten teacher in teaching and recording her student's use of scissors.*

Scissor cutting checklist:
Behavior criteria

Yes	No	Sometimes		
___	___	___	1.	Child places thumb and second finger in correct scissor holes.
___	___	___	2.	Child uses first finger as a lever to guide scissor opening and closing.
___	___	___	3.	Child opens and shuts scissors repeatedly.
___	___	___	4.	Child holds arm (elbow) tightly to the body.
___	___	___	5.	Child places scissors perpendicular to the paper.
___	___	___	6.	Child holds paper in the opposite hand, firmly, at the top of the paper. Not near the cutting line.
___	___	___	7.	Child makes cutting motions in succession. One scissor opening and closing. Ex. cutting fringe.
___	___	___	8.	Child moves scissors ahead into the paper, making 2-3 openings and closings.
___	___	___	9.	Child cuts on lines through a 4"-×-8" paper strip.

___	___	___	10.	Child cuts longer straight lines.
___	___	___	11.	Child cuts across an 8"-×-10" paper in an X shape, making four triangles.
___	___	___	12.	Child cuts straight lines of large shapes: triangle, rectangle, and square. The shapes fill the paper.
___	___	___	13.	Child cuts out a large circle shape.

*We thank Jeanne Wenzel for providing this sample task analysis.

Assignment

Attempt to task-analyze some complex skills. Choose skills from at least ~~two~~ one
content areas so you will have practice with different kinds of tasks. Some
sample tasks you might choose are:

> Locating a number in a telephone book
> Making change for sums less than 25¢, 50¢, or $1.
> Solving word problems involving addition
> Measuring by inches (or by meters) using a ruler
> Telling time by the hour and half-hour
> Lacing a shoe
> Filling out a check and stub
> Cutting with a knife and fork
> ✓ Setting a table
> Using a table of contents
> Dividing by two-digit numbers
> Solving for area of triangle, circle, etc.
> Addressing envelopes
> Using vending machines
> Playing "Fish" or "Old Maid"

Interview a Teacher

Ask someone to recommend a teacher in your area who does an exemplary job
working in a mainstream or special education classroom. Interview that teacher
to find out how he or she individualizes instruction within that setting. Find
out what teaching techniques, materials, daily schedule, activities, learning
centers, and so on, seem to be most effective. If possible, arrange to observe
the classroom in action. Record your findings below:

_____

_____

_____

_____

_____

_____

_____

_____

Developing a Learning Packet

In mainstreamed classrooms, teachers need to develop teaching techniques that are sensitive to the ability levels of individual students. The learning packet approach is especially useful because learning packets can be completed independently and because they make use of alternative learning approaches. For example, in a learning packet designed to teach students about map making, students might complete the objectives through various alternative activities such as:

    *Reading about map making
    *Constructing a map
    *Visiting a weather station
    *Viewing a filmstrip
    *Doing library research on historical maps
    *Listening to a tape on map making

These activities are appropriate for children having a range of intellectual, motor, and perceptual characteristics.

Construct and/or develop a plan for a learning packet that could be used to individualize instruction in a mainstreamed elementary school classroom. Use the outline below as a planning guide. You may select from the following topics or select one of your own.

Suggested topics

Countries in Europe, Africa, etc.
Writing a newspaper article
Writing a book report
Puppetry
Travel in Pennsylvania, etc.
Famous Americans, scientists,
  musicians, etc.
Parts of plants

Plant reproduction
Factories and assembly lines
Pollution
Space travel
Balloons and airships
Travel by ship
Babysitting/Child care
Preparing and using a personal budget

Learning Package Outline

1. Title

2. Instructional objectives

3. Teacher instructions (materials needed, how to use the package within a unit or a subject area, etc.)

4. <u>Instructions to students</u> (consider whether work is to be done individually or in groups, materials to be used, provisions for teacher feedback, use of pretests and posttests)

5. <u>Pretest</u> (You may or may not choose to use a pretest. If so, students are to take it and record their scores before beginning the packet. If any students pass the pretest, they should go on to a more advanced learning packet. Pretests are most useful, then, when a sequence of packets is being used.)

6. <u>Alternative activities for accomplishing objective</u> (Design at least five activities, remembering that each of them should meet the stated instructional objectives. Use a separate instructional sheet for each activity. Your instructions should be very clear so that students can proceed independently.)

7. <u>Posttest</u> (The posttest should measure accomplishment of the stated objectives. In some cases it may be a typical written test. In others, the student product resulting from one of the learning activities may be used as the posttest. For example, if one activity required the student to collect and label various edible wild plants, you could assess accomplishment of objectives—such as student will collect at least ten different edible wild plants, student will correctly identify 100% of plants located—by checking the finished product (the plant collection). For other packets, posttests such as presentations to a group, a reaction paper, a taped interview, and so on, may be appropriate.)

Collecting Materials for Learning Centers

One important way that the learning center approach differs from the traditional classroom is that the first provides manipulable materials. We know that children, young and old, learn by doing. We know that many children with learning problems such as hyperactivity are more goal-directed and attentive when they have something to manipulate as they learn. Learning centers provide diverse materials and activities to make learning an active, vital experience for children.

As you ponder what materials—school supplied, free and inexpensive, and so on—would be appropriate for centers, why not enlist help from some children? Children enjoy playing the game Categories. In this game, someone selects the category (e.g., "Things you can take on a picnic"). Then everyone takes turns naming an item in that category until the category is exhausted. In playing this game, you might suggest categories such as "Things I wish I were allowed to play with," "Things I could build with." Write or tape-record children's responses. Review the list, noting which of their suggestions are possible. Don't disregard them too quickly! For example, a first grader might wish to play with a record player—and it may be possible to obtain a broken one through a community or school bulletin. In playing this game with older children, you can make responses more challenging by using alphabetical ordering. For example, if the children are naming materials that can be put into the science center, they first name those that start with A, then B, etc.

Record children's suggestions below:

_____

_____

_____

_____

_____

_____

_____

Designing a Learning Center

Learning centers are typically thought of as areas set aside in classrooms to facilitate learning in given curricular areas. In a preschool class, you might find learning centers for fine motor skills, language development, creative play, and so on. In an intermediate classroom, you might instead see science, health, social studies, and reading centers. Although most centers seem to focus on content areas (e.g., science, mathematics), this need not always be so. You might have centers organized, for example, around holidays, units of study, hobbies, current events. Centers might also serve different purposes. They may be designed specifically for skill practice or for enrichment and exploratory purposes.

Teachers who work with special needs children find that learning centers can be of great assistance in individualizing and carrying out educational goals. Learning centers provide children with opportunities to learn:

    *Independent, self-directed behaviors
    *Cooperation within small groups
    *Enjoyment in skills practice
    *Enjoyment in exploratory activities
    *Generalization of skills previously taught during lessons

In the two centers on the next page, we see an example of (a) a skills building center and (b) an enrichment center.

a)

b)

In the following space, design a learning center. You may choose one with a purpose of skills practice or one for enrichment purposes. Follow the outline suggested here.

1. Center name:

2. Overall purpose (skill or enrichment):

3. Specific objectives:

4. Grade level:

5. Center rules:

6. How will children's work/progress be recorded?

7. Materials (equipment, supplies, arrangement):

8. Activities available:

9. Sketch of center:

10. Description of how the center is appropriate for children with a wide range of educational needs and characteristics:

_____

_____

_____

_____

_____

_____

_____

_____

Using Games for Practicing Skills

The retention (remembering) of many children with learning problems is greatly enhanced by overlearning. In individualizing for these children, then, the teacher needs to provide plenty of opportunities for the children to practice the content he or she teaches. (Note that games are used <u>after</u> instruction!) These children must overlearn such content as computational skills, vocabulary recognition, spelling words, dates and events, concept recognition, and so on.

Since drill can become very tedious, many teachers prefer to use game formats to provide students with skills practice. Games can be placed in subject learning centers or in a game or library center. They may be used individually or in groups.

Games that can be used for a variety of content matter are especially good to have since teachers can quickly adapt them and children need not learn many different sets of game rules.

The following are suggestions for game formats. Select or adapt one of these ideas or invent your own, construct the game, write out directions for playing, and list the possible educational content for which the game can be used.

Format 1: Lotto

Lotto games use matrix-type boards on which words, pictures, numbers, or whatever are randomly placed. Each player receives one of these boards. Accompanying the game is a stack of cards matching the concepts on the boards and of equal size. The stack should contain a match for each of the items on each of the lotto cards. For example, if three of the four lotto cards have pictures of a lion, the accompanying card stack must contain three pictures of a lion. Children take turns picking up cards from the stack and identifying them. If the child also has that item on his or her board, he or she places the card over the item on the board. If not, the card goes to the bottom of the stack. Play continues until one person fills an entire card.

6	9	8	10
1	12	4	3
16	15	7	20
17	2	18	5

1	19	18	12
15	2	6	5
16	12	3	13
7	14	17	4

7

Lotto game for practicing number recognition, numbers 1-20.

Format 2: Concentration

In Concentration, the players (usually one to four) take turns turning over concept cards that have been arranged face down in matrix formation. There are two of each card, and the object of the game is to find a pair. To do this, the players must concentrate on every attempt in order to remember where specific cards are. When a match is found, the player removes those two cards. The player with the most cards at the game's end is the winner.

As with Lotto, any concepts can be used for this game. You may play with as few as ten pairs of concepts or with many more, depending on the "concentration" skills of your students. See next page for illustration.

Format 3: Board Games

Board games are usually designed for two to six players, or for teams, as in the following game. Players compete to see who will get his or her token around the board first. Spinners, dice, or card draws are used to determine the number of moves to be made on each play. Rewards and/or penalties may be built into these games also. For example, a board game may have a small number of red and green squares randomly distributed on it. Players landing on those squares must take the same color card from the red or green card stock. Green cards might offer a bonus, such as "Move forward one space"; red cards might mean a penalty, such as "Answer this question ($3 \times 25 = ?$) or move back one space."

Concentration Game for Practicing Identification of Local Trees

Board games can be constructed so players, in order to stay at each stop, are asked to answer questions, recognize concepts, and so on. Squares on a permanent board can be covered with different items in order to change the purpose of the game. These changeable items can be attached with such things as velcro, paper clips, picture fasteners.

Board games may be designed around themes of favorite sports (such as baseball), movies (a current science fiction thriller), and so on.

Format 4: Picture Completion Games

Young children often like games in which they get to keep something. You might construct picture completion games for them, in which each correct answer earns the child an additional picture component. These are especially popular at holiday time. The following are examples.

1. Each player is given a construction paper pumpkin. As children answer questions correctly, they earn construction paper eyes, nose, mouth, eyebrows, stem, and so on. At the game's end, they can paste on the parts and keep their jack-o-lanterns.

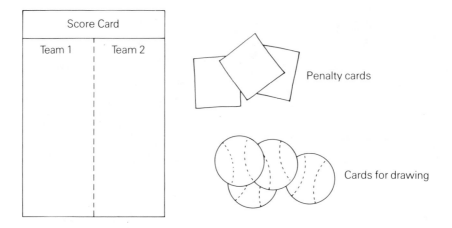

Score Card

Team 1 | Team 2

Penalty cards

Cards for drawing

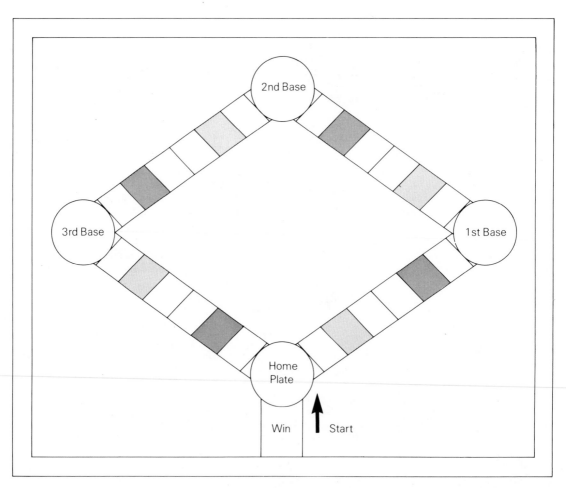

2nd Base

3rd Base

1st Base

Home
Plate

Win   Start

2. Each player is given the torso of a skeleton. With each correct answer they earn additional bones (such as skull, thigh, foot). At the game's end they are given paper fasteners to construct their skeletons.

3. Each player is given a green paper tree. Correct answers earn cut-out decorations.

4. Players begin with baskets and earn eggs, or flowers, to paste inside.

5. Players are given paper doll form, and earn pieces of clown costume.

Other formats

For other ideas, search local game stores, look at popular TV game shows—and don't forget old favorites: "fish" card game, racing to targets, spelling bees, and so on.

Evaluating Teaching Materials

According to the principle of normalization, teachers should instruct handicapped children using teaching techniques and materials that are as close as possible to those used for normal children. Teachers attempting to implement normalization practices, then, should develop skills in evaluating teaching materials to determine their appropriateness for handicapped learners.

Often you can get the best perspective on the appropriateness of certain programs or materials by carefully examining the teacher's guide. In the teacher's guide we find information about objectives, teaching techniques, use of materials, recommended grouping strategies, evaluation strategies, and so on. Visit a curriculum materials center or examine materials in your own school. Select two or three teaching programs, materials, kits; evaluate each one in terms of its appropriateness for children with these kinds of handicapping conditions:

1. Auditory impairment

2. Visual impairment

3. Mild mental retardation

4. Physical disabilities

5. Emotional disturbance

6. Learning disability, especially in reading

Make out a checklist to use in evaluating the materials. This will help you focus on characteristics such as:

1. Durability of materials

2. Specificity of objectives

3. Specificity of teaching directions

4. Use of diagnostic approach in the placement and evaluation of students in the program

5. Dimensions of learning on which the program focuses

6. Independence/dependence required in using program

7. Feedback provided

Before implementing educational intervention programs to remediate specific learning problems, you must observe the behavior. Two important reasons for this observation are:

1. To find the possible cause(s) of the problem

2. To determine the current strength of the behavior

With these observational data, teachers can then decide on instructional goals and strategies.

Part 1

For each of the following learner descriptions, answer these questions:

1. What might be causing the problem?

2. What kinds of observational data would best tell you the current strengths of the problem?

Learner Description A

Mary is a seven-year-old child who is still on a readiness level in reading. She has begun to learn some sound symbols and does well at recognizing these during one-to-one instructional sessions. When she is given a workbook or independent reading assignments, however, she does nothing or just raises her hand for help. She makes no progress except when you are with her. You are quite concerned as you can spend only 5 to 10 minutes daily with Mary's reading, and she is falling further behind.

_____

_____

_____

_____

_____

_____

Learner Description B

Harry is a very active child. He learns well when you are able to capture his attention, but he is easily distracted and his constant movement often bothers the other children. He is in the fifth grade and about a year behind on most skill subjects. His intellectual ability is normal on standardized tests. You would like to teach Harry to control his activity level, however, since it interferes with his learning and influences his peers.

_____

_____

_____

_____

_____

_____

Learner Description C

John is a third grader who has had difficulty in acquiring reading skills since he began school. He can read, but makes many errors and asks for a lot of assistance. One of his most common error patterns occurs when he reads only the first one or two letters of the word and guesses the rest from context clues. For example, he read "tree" for trap.

_____

_____

_____

_____

_____

_____

Learner Description D

Cathy is a fourth grader. You are having difficulty teaching her handwriting. She can make all the appropriate letter formations, but her writing is very slow. She takes at least twice as much time as the rest of the class as she carefully forms each letter.

_____

_____

_____

_____

_____

Learner Description E

Jenny is a sixth grader who has always had some difficulty with math. Her computational skills are on a fourth-grade level. She can do rote-type problems, but often doesn't understand arithmetic concepts, why certain processes are used, and so on. And she still cannot solve story problems other than those involving simple addition. She adds when presented with any word problem.

_____

_____

_____

_____

_____

_____

_____

Part 2

In this section you will be given data on some of the children you have just read about. Based on these data:

1. Write an appropriate annual goal (long-term objective) and a beginning level short-term objective.

2. Describe the teaching strategy or strategies you would use to accomplish the short-term objective.

Learner B

After observing Harry's hyperactivity for a few days, the teacher began to notice somewhat of a pattern. Harry often became distracted when in a situation in which he was not being rewarded or in one that was difficult for him. The teacher, therefore, designed a data collection sheet that gave her both frequency and situational information about Harry's distractability.

Class periods	Number of distractions	What happened prior to/ during distractions
45 min. math	~~IIII~~ ~~IIII~~ II	given worksheets that were difficult; problems marked wrong
30 min. social studies	~~IIII~~	discussion of reading assignment
30 min. art	1	happened before materials were passed out
45 min. reading	~~IIII~~	all happened during independent assignment

Learner C

John's teacher collected data on all words that he mispronounced during 4- and 5-minute oral reading samples that were at the second-grade level. Below is a representative list of her findings:

Word	Mispronunciation
bet	bit
trap	tree
sheet	shell
plan	plate
heat	hat
send	sent
cut	cat
pin	pan
whip	when

Section D: Writing Individualized Education Programs

A Word to Our Readers

The federal government has set down certain requirements for educating handicapped children in Public Law 94-142, The Education for All Handicapped Children Act of 1975* This federal law requires that all state and local education
agencies have annual program plans that specify, in detail, how the agencies
will follow the federal law.

The activities that follow relate generally to the federal law. However, you
should obtain a copy of your state regulations if you are interested in seeing
how your state complies with federal mandates. If you are responsible for
planning and implementing Individualized Education Programs (IEPs), you should
be sure to have copies of state and local guidelines.

You may want to consult an introductory level textbook in special education
such as Educating Special Learners by G. Phillip Cartwright, Carol Cartwright,
and Marjorie Ward (published by Wadsworth Publishing Company in 1981) for additional information about P.L. 94-142 and the roles and responsibilities of
teachers in implementing the law.

Become Familiar with IEP Guidelines

Obtain a copy of your state's guidelines on P.L. 94-142, as well as any guidelines on the development of IEPs. Obtain IEP forms used by your local school
district. Compare the forms with the guidelines. Do the forms comply clearly
with the guidelines? Record any questions you have in completing this assignment. Meet with the local IEP coordinator, your supervisor, instructor, or
other involved person to clear up your questions.

Participating on the Evaluation Team

Consider the roles of the special education and the regular classroom teacher
on the IEP evaluation team. Assume that you are developing a plan for a learning disabled student who currently spends one hour per day with the resource
teacher, working on reading skills. The child is a third grader but reads at a

*You can obtain a copy of the Law and Regulations for P.L. 94-142 from your
congressional representative.

first-grade level. The child's functioning is at grade level in content areas where reading is not emphasized.

What kinds of formal and informal assessment measures should both teachers use in order to contribute to the evaluation? What special areas of information should the regular class teacher emphasize in his or her evaluation? What resources did you find most helpful in deciding on your evaluation methods?

Writing the Educational Plan

The IEP forms containing the annual goals and plans for teaching and evaluating the short-term objectives are the core of the IEP. It is important that teachers be skilled in writing this aspect of the individualized education program.

Refer to the three child descriptions from the activity on adjusting instructional objectives (pp. 85-88). Choose one of these children and select three appropriate annual goals for him or her. For each annual goal, fill out an IEP using the form on the following page. As you complete this assignment, remember that:

1.   Short-term objectives should be small steps that lead to the completion of the annual goal. You may need to task-analyze the annual goal.

2.   Methods and materials you select should be related to learning characteristics of the child.

3.   Evaluation methods and criteria should be specific and also relate to characteristics of the child's behavior.

Assess Your Competencies in IEP Development

Obtain a copy of P.L. 94-142 or your state's guidelines for IEP development. As you read the components, make a list of competencies a teacher needs to have to develop and implement good IEPs. Use a rating scale or some other manner of assessment to indicate your own skills in each area of competency you have indicated. How might you develop competencies in your areas of weakness (take pertinent courses, practicum experiences, independent study, and so on)?

Instructional Area:

Annual Goals:

Short-Term Objective	Instructional Methods Media/Material Title(s) (Optional)	Evaluation of Instructional Objectives	
		Tests, Materials Evaluation Procedures To Be Used	Criteria of Successful Performance

Using the IEP for Parent Conferences

P.L. 94-142 requires that parents be presented with the procedures and results of their child's evaluation and that the parents participate in the IEP meeting. IEPs, then, are to be evaluated and revised <u>at least</u> once a year (many districts conduct the review at the beginning of each new school year).

In most school districts, regular classroom teachers schedule one or two parent conferences during each school year. These may be individual parent meetings, home visits, or group meetings. Teachers might use these meetings as opportunities to review children's progress on IEPs and to build parent-school interactions so that IEP meetings can proceed smoothly with a minimum of misunderstandings when they do occur officially.

Outline a format for an individual parent conference and one for a parent group meeting that includes attention to a child's IEP progress. Think how you might manage the parent group meeting so you protect the confidentiality of any particular child's educational program. What kinds of information might parents want to know <u>during</u> the year? What materials should the teacher prepare for the conference?

Critiquing Evaluation Devices

P.L. 94-142 states that children will be evaluated in a nondiscriminatory manner; specifically, the guidelines* state that:

1. Tests and other evaluation materials
    a. Are provided and administered in the child's native language or other mode of communication, unless it is clearly not feasible to do so;
    b. Have been validated for the specific purpose for which they are used; and
    c. Are administered by trained personnel in conformance with the instructions provided by their producer;

2. Tests and other evaluation materials include those tailored to assess specific areas of educational need and not merely those which are designed to provide a single general intelligence quotient;

3. Tests are selected and administered so as best to ensure that when a test is administered to a child with impaired sensory, manual or speaking skills, the test results accurately reflect the child's aptitude or achievement level or whatever other factors the test purports to measure, rather than reflecting the child's impaired sensory, manual, or speaking skills (except where those skills are the factors which the test purports to measure);

*Federal Register, August 23, 1977, pp. 42496-42497.

4. No single procedure is used as the sole criterion for determining an appropriate educational program for a child; and

5. The evaluation is made by a multidisciplinary team or group of persons, including at least one teacher or other specialist with knowledge in the area of suspected disability;

6. The child is assessed in all areas related to suspected disability including where appropriate, health, vision, hearing, social and emotional status, general intelligence, academic performance, communicative status and motor abilities.

Your Assignment

Choose two norm-referenced assessment devices currently used in your school district or in your special area of education (e.g., reading, early childhood education). You might want to choose one intelligence measure and one achievement measure. Critique them according to the evaluation guidelines for 94-142. What recommendations can you make concerning the usefulness of these measures? In what ways might those measures discriminate against children with these kinds of handicapping conditions: mentally retarded, emotionally disturbed, sensory impaired, language impaired, physically handicapped, health-impaired, learning disabled?

Section E: Tips on Integrating Handicapped Children

Activities for the Beginning of the Year

Often teachers can prevent social interaction problems between handicapped and nonhandicapped children by seeing that all children get to know each other as individuals at the beginning of the year. A number of activities can help with this. Try to add some of your own after reading the following. Share your ideas!

Activity: Body tracing

Objectives: To have children take time to attend to and tell of positive attributes of one another.

Materials: large roll of newsprint, crayons or markers, large floor space

Procedures: Children lie flat on floor while teacher or peer traces around them. Instead of coloring in the form, have children write at least three things about themselves inside the form. When all are done, take turns showing pictures and sharing the three statements with classmates. Ask other students to contribute positive comments to pictures being shared.

Are there any handicapped children for whom this activity would be inappropriate? How could you adjust the activity to suit this child's needs?

Activity: Making a coat of arms

Objectives: To provide an experience in which children can learn about one
            another's family.

Materials: construction paper, markers, copy machine, pictures of coats of
            arms

Procedures: Begin with a discussion of families. Ask children to tell about
            their families—how many members, favorite activities, favorite
            foods, hobbies, collections, pets, and so on.

            Explain that a coat of arms depicts characteristics of families.
            Show and explain some coats of arms. Ask the children to design
            a coat of arms for their families, depicting some of the charac-
            teristics discussed earlier.

            For a follow-up activity, make copies of each child's product.
            Have children show and tell about their coats of arms. Then pass
            out the copies, with names blocked out. Ask children to guess
            whose they have. Children may be given several to guess; tally
            their correct score at the end.

Activity: My first day

Objectives: To help new children feel more comfortable by hearing others
            tell stories about their first day at school. To sensitize other
            children to the feelings and needs of children spending their
            first days in a new classroom.

Materials: None

Procedures: Teacher begins the discussion by reminding children that some
            classmates are in that class for the first time. The teacher
            then tells a story about his or her first day somewhere, such as
            the first day he or she ever taught school, went to college, and
            so on. Try to choose an incident that is both humorous and shows
            some of the emotion felt on a "first day." Ask students to share
            their first day experience. End discussion by assuring new stu-
            dents that everyone will understand and help them through any
            mishaps they encounter!

Activity: Incomplete sentences

Objectives: To provide a nonthreatening situation in which all children can
               contribute to a group discussion. To provide an opportunity to
               learn emotional characteristics of one another.

Materials: Incomplete sentence stems, written in large print for class, or
               on lesson plan for teacher, tape recorder (optional)

Procedures: Ask class to sit in a circle so it will be easy for them to take
               turns answering. Explain that one way to get to know one an-
               other is to play the Incomplete Sentence Game. Give an example
               of a sentence stem and answer. Choose sentence stems that you
               think are most appropriate for your class. Include some that are
               humorous, as this helps keep children's attention. Some sentence
               stems are suggested below:

               1. When I am out of school _____.

               2. When I am mad _____.

               3. When I am sad about something _____.

               4. I think school _____.

               5. What really makes me happy is _____.

               6. I get quiet when _____.

               7. I like people who _____.

               8. If I could have one wish _____.

Follow-up: A. After the activity, discuss ways in which we are all alike,
                   all different. How can we use such information to better
                   understand each other?

               B. You might wish to tape or otherwise record children's re-
                   sponses at the beginning of the year, then do the activity
                   again at the middle or end of the year. Discuss ways in
                   which children have changed, why, and so on.

Work alone, or with a group, to design at least two more activities to facilitate integration of the handicapped.

Activity:

Objectives:

Materials:

Procedures:

Activity:

Objectives:

Materials:

Procedures:

Developing Sensitivity in Nonhandicapped Children

Until recently, most public school children had limited experiences with their handicapped peers. Segregated instructional practices led to many poor attitudes and behaviors among nonhandicapped children: fear of those who are different, name-calling and teasing, pitying, ignoring, and so on.

In order to make children sensitive to the effects their behavior has on handicapped children, devise sensitivity games and use them, especially at the beginning of the school year. One special educator has suggested a game called Words and Phrases That Hurt* for teaching race and ethnic relations. This game might be adapted to needs in a mainstreamed educational setting. In a simple version of this game, players gather around a stack of cards containing words and phrases directed toward a handicapped person. Players alternate in turning up cards, reading them, and telling whether the words or phrases would hurt and why. Finally, the whole group discusses a better response. If the group finds a more appropriate response than the words or phrase that hurt, they may go on to the next card. Two or more groups may be formed for the game, and the group that solves the most problems wins.

Assignment

Within your work group, make up an assortment of fifteen to twenty cards for using this game in a mainstreamed elementary school. Try to make the incidents on the cards as realistic as possible. In fact, you may want to observe in an elementary school before completing the assignment.

Some examples from the game devised for racial and ethnic awareness are:

1. A white person to a black person: "Your people are so happy all the time."

2. To an Italian person: "Why, you don't look Italian!"

3. A teacher, about poor children: "If we let them take the books home, they'll just get them dirty and destroy them."

Adjusting Your Daily Schedule

Children being mainstreamed in regular classrooms do need extra support from the teacher. Often mainstreaming doesn't work because teachers neglect to plan extra time to work with the handicapped children and time to see that the children do integrate.

*In Charlotte Epstein, Classroom Management and Teaching: Persistent Problems and Rational Solutions (Reston, Va.: Reston Publishing Co., 1979), pp. 144-148.

For this activity, choose a particular grade level and a typical daily schedule. Assume that two children are being mainstreamed in that class. One child has a moderate hearing impairment, uses a hearing aid, uses speech, but has articulation problems. The other child is about two years behind in academic subjects. What kinds of special assistance might these children need from the regular class teacher? How much extra time do you think should be given to these children? (They do spend time daily with a special teacher.) Who should give the extra time—teacher, classroom aide, other students? Revise the daily schedule to accommodate the needs of the two mainstreamed children.

Fostering Social Integration

In many mainstreamed settings, we see handicapped and nonhandicapped children integrated physically (they are in the same classes), but not socially (they do not play, talk together). Teachers can foster social interaction by choosing activities that <u>require</u> cooperation among children. If such activities are commonly used at the beginning of the school year, nonhandicapped children may not learn to exclude their handicapped peers from activities. Some examples of activities in which children must cooperate and interact are the Hot Potato Game, conducting interviews for a classroom newsletter, and so on.

In the space below, list and describe as many activities as you can that encourage all children to interact.

_____

_____

_____

_____

_____

_____

_____

_____

_____

_____

_____

Role-Playing

In this activity, children dramatize problems and their possible solutions. Role-playing can be used quite effectively to solve problems one might encounter in mainstream situations. Many special education teachers use it to prepare handicapped children for their integration experiences. They have children dramatize their reactions to both negative and positive incidents—for example, when children tease them, if they don't understand instructions, finding something to say to new classmates on the first day of school. Regular class teachers use role-playing to help their students see things from the point of view of the exceptional children being integrated. The children can also use role-playing to practice positive interactions with children whose behaviors may present some difficulties (such as hyperactivity, aggression).

Typically, role-playing activities have four components:

1. Children and teacher—the problem situation(s), focusing on the specific incidents of concern. For example, when discussing the problem of being teased, encourage children to tell the specifics—what did someone say or do while teasing.

2. Students are assigned to roles and act out one of the specific situations discussed. The rest of the class watches attentively.

3. All students, observers and participants, discuss and analyze the incident. Students are encouraged to analyze people's behaviors both affectively (how must someone have felt?) and cognitively (what would have been a better thing to do?). Students then decide how the incident might be changed to provide more suitable outcomes. Here they must be specific, considering how one should behave, speak, and so on.

4. Finally the incident is reenacted, this time with the actors behaving according to the groups' decisions about the most appropriate behaviors.

This activity should enhance children's acquisition of positive interaction skills in two ways:

1. Children acting out parts can actually rehearse and be rewarded for desirable behaviors. This kind of positive practice is especially good for children who need to learn techniques to control their social behaviors. At times, then, the teacher may select certain children to be actors because they need this opportunity for positive practice.

2. Children watching the dramatization and participating in the discussions can learn appropriate behaviors through observation.

Assignment

Select a given grade level—one you are familiar with—and list a number of role-playing topics or situations that might help both normal and handicapped children adjust better to mainstream settings.

Consider how you can ensure that children will continue to practice the positive behaviors they learn during the role-playing activities. Some suggestions are: make certain the teacher is observant and reinforcing of these behaviors, have children keep diaries of interpersonal objectives and their own behaviors, make posters which everyone in class can see. Do you have other suggestions?

Big Brother/Big Sister Program

One way to make the newly integrated handicapped child feel more comfortable is to assign each new class member (whether handicapped, a transfer child, or whatever) a big brother/or big sister from the class. These persons are responsible for interacting with the new children, helping them find their way about the school, making friends, and so on. It should be quite an honor to be asked to be a big brother/or big sister. The teacher might meet with this group weekly for the first few months of school to talk about how the new children are adjusting socially, what activities were successful in enhancing social interaction, and so on.

Prepare an outline for a one-hour training session for the big brother/big sister group prior to their assignments. Make your content appropriate for a primary, intermediate, or secondary grade level.

Reading Selections and Attitudes Toward the Handicapped

Most teachers are not themselves handicapped and do not have handicapped members in their immediate families. All of us, whether teachers or students, can enhance our understanding and attitudes toward handicapped persons through literature.

Select and read a book on the life of a handicapped person, on the experiences of his/or her family, and so on. Many of these are listed in the resources section of this book. Keep a record of your reactions. Based on how your reading experience affected you, plan a reading unit for a classroom. Go to your library and consult book lists to identify suitable books for children to read. Write a summary sentence or two for each book, noting reading level. List and describe several which children might read during this reading unit. Share your book lists and activities with others.

Learning About Handicaps

The next two activities are suggested in the book, *Clarification of P.L. 94-142 For the Classroom Teacher (published by Research for Better Schools, 444 North Third Street, Philadelphia, Pa., 1978, pp. 20-26). The activities are suggested for use by regular class teachers who wish to prepare their students for mainstreaming. Basically, the purposes of these activities are to make the children more familiar with handicapped persons, to expose them to both facts and myths about the handicapped, and to help develop mature, normalizing attitudes toward the handicapped.

Activity 1: Films

Show your students one or more of the following films. The age group suggested as appropriate for each film is given. At the end of the films have a follow-up discussion. Questions might relate to particular problems the film focused on, ways to solve those problems, comparison between the community shown in the film and its dynamics and one's own community, discussion of specific vocabulary used in the film (such as dyslexia, hyperactivity, quadriplegia), personal reactions, and so on.

Being—21 minutes/color/1973/A.C.I. Films Inc.
  A young man, paralyzed in both legs, confuses friendship for pity.
  (intermediate/secondary)

Child of the Universe—30 minutes/color/1973/Robin Miller.
  The fears and suspicions of the retarded. A commentary by parents of the
  mentally retarded and retarded adults in society. (intermediate/
  secondary)

The Curb Between Us—15 minutes/color/1975/Arthur Barr Productions.
  A disabled adolescent as he rebuilds his life after an accident.
  (intermediate/secondary)

A Day in the Life of Bonnie Consolo—16½ minutes/color/1975/Arthur Barr Productions.
  How a woman without arms manages her life, showing her ingenious self-
  sufficiency. (secondary)

Even Love Is Not Enough—color/1975/Parents Magazine Films, Inc.
  A collection of four sets of filmstrips: Behavioral and Emotional Disabilities, Physical Disabilities, Intellectual Disabilities, and Educational and Language Disabilities. Each set contains five full-color
  filmstrips, either a long-playing record or cassettes, script books,
  and a discussion guide.

*Reprinted by permission.

The Exceptional Child—51 minutes/black and white/1967/BBC-Time-Life Films.
    Bright to less gifted special students and how they cope in school.
    (secondary)

He Comes from Another Room—28 minutes/color/1973/National Audiovisual
    Center.
    The transition of two emotionally disturbed students to regular classes
    in the third grade. (secondary)

The Invisible Handicap— 15 minutes/color/1976/Carousel Films.
    A "60 Minute" program on problems of learning disabilities.
    (intermediate/secondary)

Leo Beuerman—13 minutes/color/1969/Centron.
    How a man, physically handicapped since birth, overcame adversity; his
    philosophy of life. (intermediate/secondary)

Like Other People—37 minutes/color/1973/Perennial Education.
    A narration of the social, emotional, and sexual needs of physically
    handicapped young people. (secondary)

A Matter of Inconvenience—10 minutes/color/1974/Stanfield House.
    How blind and amputee individuals refuse to accept stereotypes. Illus-
    trates the difference between a disability and a handicap. (intermediate/
    secondary)

Mimi—12 minutes/black and white/1972/Billy Budd Films.
    A young paralyzed woman's account of her life and how she relates to
    others. (intermediate/secondary)

Not Without Sight—19 minutes/color/1973/American Foundation for the Blind.
    Defines major types of visual impairments and their causes; shows the
    world through the eyes of several types. (intermediate/secondary)

Readin' and Writin' Ain't Everything—26 minutes/color/1975/Stanfield House.
    The personal accounts of young mentally retarded adults and three fami-
    lies with mentally retarded children; emphasizes the need for acceptance
    and understanding. (secondary)

Sit Down, Shut Up, or Get Out—58 minutes/color/1971/Films, Inc.
    A bright kid with behavior problems reacts with his parents/teacher/
    peers. (intermediate/secondary)

Some of Our Schoolmates are Blind—20 minutes/color/1960/Hollywood Film
    Enterprises.
    A public elementary school that includes blind students. (intermediate/
    secondary)

They Call Me Names—22 minutes/color/1972/BFA Educational Media.
How mentally deficient young people perceive a world in which they are
told they are "different." (intermediate/secondary)

Triumph of Christy Brown—60 minutes/black and white/1971/Indiana University.
An Irish author and painter and the cerebral palsy handicap he overcame.
(intermediate/secondary)

Activity 2: Research Report

Give students a list of handicapped persons both living and dead. Ask each
student to select one of these persons, to research his or her life, and to
present a report (either oral or written). The report might include:

a. The nature and cause of the person's handicapping condition

b. How the handicap affected the person's functioning in various aspects
of life

c. What the person's accomplishments were

d. What some of the emotions felt by the person and his or her family were

Some handicapped persons on whom students might do research reports:

Artists

Ludwig van Beethoven, deaf
Elizabeth Barrett Browning,
   spinal injuries (bedridden)
Ray Charles, blind
Jose Feliciano, blind

Aldous Huxley, blind
James Stacey, amputee (arm/leg)
Stevie Wonder, blind
Al Capp, amputee (leg)

Athletes

Dave Bing, blind (one eye)
Tom Dempsey, birth defect
   (stump foot and arm)

Carlos May, minus a thumb
Roy Campanella, paralyzed (neck down)
Wilma Rudolph, childhood polio

Politicians

Winston Churchill, speech
   impediment
Robert Dole, withered arm
David Inouye, amputee (arm)
Franklin D. Roosevelt, paralyzed
   (both legs)

Morris Udall, blind (one eye)
George Wallace, paralyzed (waist down)
Nelson Rockefeller (learning disabled)

Inventors/Scientist

Louis Braille, blind
Thomas Edison, deaf

Peer Tutoring

The peer tutoring techniques that many teachers have been using recently are especially well suited to mainstream educational settings. Peer tutoring has many advantages; among them are:

1. It results in interaction between normal and handicapped children.

2. Children who have recently learned certain content themselves often have insights into how to teach it based on their learning experiences.

3. It makes learning less competitive and more cooperative.

4. It provides experiences in caring and being cared for, such as we hope to teach as part of living in a democracy.

Successful peer teaching programs must be well planned. Teachers must decide:

1. How to choose the tutors and tutees (Will they be same-age or cross-age tutors?)

2. How to work the peer tutoring into the classroom schedule and space

3. How to train the tutors

Some potential problems that might arise with such a system are:

1. A child who always needs extra help may feel singled out.

2. The tutors may feel uneasy about assuming the role of "teacher."

3. The teacher may have difficulty keeping track of progress and problems during tutoring sessions.

Visit a classroom, obtain a copy of the schedule, and diagram the space and classroom arrangement. Develop a plan for peer tutoring that would be workable there. Include the three decision areas, but plan to avoid the three problem areas.

Visit a classroom in which peer tutoring is used. Write up your observations, noting how that teacher deals with the three decision areas and three problem areas.

Assessing Your Skills

The self-report inventory that follows* was developed by the New York University Resource Access Project (a federally funded effort to help Head Start teachers integrate handicapped children into Head Start programs). Most of the items apply to other educational programs, too.

Complete the inventory as honestly as you can. When you finish, look back over your responses, paying special attention to items you marked 4.

Write at least two goals for yourself to accomplish in the next six months. Include information about <u>what</u> training you need, <u>where</u> and <u>how</u> you will get it, and <u>when</u> you will do it.

The self-check inventory is designed to identify the many elements in successfully mainstreaming children with special needs. We have provided the following code for self-assessment. From this information you may be able to set goals for the coming months.

1. *I do this regularly and satisfactorily.*

2. *I do this but need to improve.*

3. *I haven't done this yet but will begin this month.*

4. *I need more training or guidance before I begin.*

<u>*The Parent-Teacher Relationship*</u>

_____ *Introduce self and all staff to new families.*

_____ *Provide a tour of the classroom and explain how and what children learn in Head Start (e.g., small-group teaching).*

_____ *Listen to parents and support their efforts to learn more about their child's learning needs and progress.*

---

*From <u>Mainstreaming in Head Start, Training Strategies for Introduction to Generic Concepts and Specific Categorical Skills of Mainstreaming</u>, developed by Judith Rothschild, Linda Kjerland, and Dinah Heller, 1978. New York University, School of Continuing Education, Office of Community Service Programs, Resource Access Project, Region II, 3 Washington Square Village, Suit 1-M, New York, NY 10012. Reprinted by permission.

_____ Listen to parents and remember that they bring information and years of experience with their child that are available for the staff in getting to know the child.

_____ Plan a visit to the center for parent and child that allows for all involved to get to know each other, ask questions, and share information.

_____ Talk together with parents about the learning needs and strengths of the child, goals to work toward, and ways to reach the goals.

_____ Exchange phone numbers and times to call that are best for both parent and teacher.

_____ Periodically discuss parent's volunteer participation changes, limits, and new interests.

_____ Periodically send activity ideas to be used at home and then follow up in how the activities went.

Individualized Planning

_____ Observe and record observations frequently beginning with the child's first day in the center.

_____ Observe in many different settings and different times of the day.

_____ Observe the child's learning style.

_____ Assess the child in all developmental areas.

_____ Use developmental information for planning.

_____ Periodically update the developmental assessment, and update plans accordingly.

_____ Task-analyze activities that are difficult for the child.

_____ Work out ways to adapt the room, routine, material, or amount of guidance to be able to change an activity from frustrating to successful for the child.

Setting Expectations and Choosing Techniques

_____ Set standards for all center staff to follow when working with the children.

_____ Make the standards work by following them yourself.

_____ *Reinforce positive behaviors and help staff improve negative behaviors toward children.*

_____ *Avoid overprotecting the child and thus limiting his or her experiences in coping with self and others.*

_____ *Set realistic expectations while you build the child's confidence.*

_____ *Use honest not exaggerated praise.*

_____ *"Send out" messages that encourage independence.*

_____ *Be honest with other children when questions arise.*

_____ *Be honest with the child while providing experiences that build the self-concept.*

_____ *Read from books and other materials to find out more when not sure about something related to a special need.*

Section F: Environmental Arrangements

Preparing Your Classroom for Handicapped Children

For the most part, you will need to make few modifications for the handicapped children you mainstream. Good environmental settings for normal learners are generally appropriate for handicapped learners, too. In this activity you will be asked to consider minor adjustments that may be necessary, however.

Begin this assignment by designing a room floor plan and labeling furniture, learning centers, blackboards, windows, and so on. Then, explain what adjustments you would consider appropriate for the following handicapping conditions:

Hearing impaired—consider enhancing visual aspects of the environment (e.g., ability to see speakers for lip reading, ability to see activities), consider noise level (will it distract a child who uses a hearing aid?).

Visually impaired—consider proximity and accessibility of materials used for independent work, whether light is appropriate for children whose eyes are photosensitive, whether traffic moves through cleared areas, whether auditory stimuli are accessible to the child.

Physically impaired—consider whether special equipment (e.g., a wheelchair) is needed and how it will fit in with other equipment (e.g., wheelchairs fitting in aisles, under desks), whether the child can reach and manipulate materials for independent work, whether traffic patterns are safe.

Designing a Playground

The playground is an important part of the school environment. Here, a great deal of socialization, learning, and exploration take place. In order to make the total school environment appropriate for all children, we must design playgrounds that are appropriate for exceptional as well as normal children. In this activity you are asked to suggest changes in an existing playground so that it will be appropriate for handicapped as well as normal children.

Use the form on p. 128. Begin by listing handicapping conditions (e.g., mental retardation, auditory impairment) that you wish to consider; choose at least three. For each handicapping condition you've chosen, note what kinds of behavioral deficits might be present (e.g., child may not recall rules for equipment

use, child may be afraid to take risks). Then visit a playground, noting the
specific problems it might present to those children; make suggestions for
changing the playground so it will be more appropriate for them. (Use form on
p. 129 for playground information.)

A. Handicapping conditions being considered   Possible behavioral deficits

1. _____   1. _____
   _____   _____
   _____   _____
   _____   _____

2. _____   2. _____
   _____   _____
   _____   _____
   _____   _____

3. _____   3. _____
   _____   _____
   _____   _____
   _____   _____

B. Layout of playground observed:

C. Possible problems detected: Recommended solutions:

Encouraging Cooperation

Many researchers who observe young children in integrated educational settings note that normal and handicapped children do not interact spontaneously
with each other. This lack of interaction is a very real problem for educators, however, since one of the main intentions of mainstream education is to
promote desirable social interactions between normal and handicapped children.

One way we can promote desirable interaction is by structuring an environment
in which cooperation is necessary or in which it enhances the enjoyment of an
activity. For example, in a preschool block area, you can include large or
heavy blocks that require at least two children for effective manipulation; on
a fine motor table, you can include games (e.g., bingo) as well as individual
tasks (such as puzzles, peg boards). Although such arrangements don't necessi-
tate interaction specifically between normal and handicapped children, they do
encourage general cooperation among children. The teacher then only needs to
arrange for the physical proximity of children and the toys and equipment will
suggest the need to cooperate.

Choose the grade level you teach or would like to teach, and look through a
school supply/equipment catalog, identifying several materials that would require or encourage cooperation among children. Consider each item carefully,
since many games may actually encourage more competition than cooperation. In
a cooperative task, the mutual activity is equally rewarding to both parties.
In games that culminate with a win, the mutual activity is not likely to be as
rewarding for the losers as for the winners. Record your choices on p. 131.

Planning Field Trips

Field trips sometimes present special problems for special education teachers.
Some community facilities are unavailable or inappropriate for children with
certain disabilities. Make a list of field trips available in your community.
Describe briefly some educational outcomes of each field trip. Note any special difficulties posed by inclusion of children having these problems: physical handicaps, auditory impairments, visual impairments, learning disabilities, emotional problems, mental retardation, speech or language disabilities.

Note also some general policies and procedures for field trips that are appropriate for the grade level you choose.

Designing Open Access Centers

Design a classroom independent learning center that would be appropriate and
accessible to all children regardless of disabilities. Draw a scaled diagram

Materials list	Supply source	Type of interaction encouraged

of the center including permanent fixtures such as tables and bulletin boards. Prepare a list of commercial and teacher-made materials for inclusion in the center. Write instructions for students' use of the center, such as number of students allowed there at one time, types of objectives accomplished there, techniques for informing students of activities and procedures available, assessment procedures. Tell why the center is equally appropriate for children with these disabilities: physical, visual, auditory, cognitive, social-emotional, language. Use the form on p. 133.

Selecting Materials and Equipment

Many school supply companies now include materials and equipment for handicapped children in their inventories. See the resources section for names of companies. Prepare a report on the types of special equipment and materials available for a specific type of disability. Describe or clip illustrations of the equipment, noting the purposes of each item, its cost, and distributor. Evaluate the items based on cost, usefulness, and appropriateness for that disability. Compare your findings with others. What is your overall assessment of school suppliers' responses to the needs of exceptional children in the schools? Do you see particular areas of strength and weakness?

Taking a Building Tour

Take a tour of a local school building and at least one classroom. Assume that you have a physical, visual, or auditory handicap. List any areas that would be inaccessible to you, areas that present difficulties, activities or other stimulation in which you could not participate, and any possible hazards. What improvements would you suggest?

Insuring Safety in a Preschool

Preschool teachers are always faced with the need to assess carefully safety aspects of their classrooms. Teachers of older children can merely set safety rules, such as that a paper cutter can only be used with adult supervision, and children comply. The preschool teacher, however, knows that children might explore any materials to which they have access, regardless of rules! Now that preschools are being integrated, the task of insuring safety in the classroom is often more difficult.

Visit a local preschool, noting what kinds of safety precautions and procedures are being used. Then consider the kinds of changes that would be necessary in order to include the following children:

Grade Level: _____

```
┌─────────────────────────────────────────────────────────────┐
│                                                             │
│                                                             │
│                                                             │
│                                                             │
│                                                             │
│                                                             │
│                                                             │
│                                                             │
│                                                             │
│                                                             │
│                                                             │
│                                                             │
└─────────────────────────────────────────────────────────────┘
```

Center Diagram

Materials: _____

_____

_____

_____

Instructions for student use: _____

_____

_____

_____

Appropriateness for handicapped children: _____

_____

_____

_____

Gregory (age 3)—This child has a mild motor handicap. He lacks finer levels
of coordination in most motor tasks—that is, he can run, but often
falls; he can pour, but not smoothly and often spills; he can color, but
with abrupt movements.

Bonnie (age 4)—Bonnie has social-emotional problems. When she has tantrums
(as often as three times a week), she often throws things such as games,
blocks.

Billy (age 3)—Billy has low vision, although he can detect large objects,
light-darkness, movement, and so on.

Prompting Self-help Skills

The teaching of self-help skills is an important component of many programs
for exceptional children. This teaching is accomplished most efficiently when
staff persons and children alike are aware of the procedures to be followed.
Prepare three model charts that might be hung at various places in a classroom that would provide procedural cues for children and staff. Try to think
of tasks other than the typical self-help skills (handwashing, hanging up
clothing, and so on). For example, you might consider one to hang in an art
center that cues children in procedures for independently using finger paint—
from preparation through clean-up. Record your ideas on p. 135.

Section G: Working With Other Professionals

Selecting Adult Information for Your Classroom Library

Imagine that you teach in a class for handicapped preschoolers. A number of adults are involved in your program, and you wish to make your professional library available to them. You would, however, like to expand your library so that your reading matter is appropriate for a variety of persons. Currently, these adults are involved in your program:

> *Center director
> *Student teachers (undergraduate)
> *Teacher's aide
> *Parents
> *Program board members
> *Speech therapist
> *Occupational therapist
> *Psychologist

While the professionals on your list are certainly competent in their specialty—speech problems, for example, they may be interested in publications that relate their area of expertise to the special characteristics of preschoolers.

Select library acquisitions relevant for each person involved, identifying at least three publications for each. You may choose from books, journals, or magazines.

Working Out Problems with Your Aide

As a special educator, you will likely have some sort of teaching assistant, student teacher, or whomever, assigned to you for at least part of the day. Often problems occur when the teacher's aide and the teacher differ as to how to handle situations.

Working with two or three other persons, identify three specific problems that may arise between a teacher and assistant. Then role-play these situations, enacting how the situation would be handled by authoritarian, democratic, and

*Adapted from an activity in Day Care: Practices and Issues by Judith Seaver and Susan Dangel (University Park, Pa.: The Pennsylvania State University, 1976). Reprinted by permission.

laissez-faire teachers. After your role-plays, discuss the pros and cons of each approach. Might different approaches be better for different situations?

Planning a Training Session for Aides

It is usually necessary to train new teacher's aides for work with exceptional children. Often these persons may have had little experience with special children, but even those who are experienced will probably need an orientation to your teaching procedures, classroom management, educational philosophy, and so on.

Plan the possible content for a training/orientation session for a new teacher's aide. You may use up to two days for the training. Outline your content, describe the interpersonal atmosphere you would strive for during those sessions, and describe what "teaching techniques" or activities you would use.

Identifying and Referring a Student

Assume that you are a third-grade teacher. You have a child in your classroom who is just at a readiness level in reading and not progressing well. Furthermore, this child is very quiet and withdrawn. You believe the child may have special educational needs and should be referred for an evaluation.

Outline the procedures you should go through in referring this student for evaluation. Be sure to refer to a copy of your state's guidelines on P.L. 94-142 in completing this assignment. Consider the kinds of data you would need to support your concern, as well as how you could collect that data.

Understanding the Principal's Role in Mainstreaming

Parents often call the principal's office to question procedures used in their children's classroom. In mainstream classrooms many teachers group normal with handicapped children. This information, when reported to a parent, can trigger a range of reactions. For example, consider this situation:

*Adapted from an activity in Clarification of P.L. 94-142 for the Classroom Teacher, published by Research for Better Schools, Inc., Philadelphia, Pa., 1978, p. 18. Reprinted by permission.
†Adapted from an activity in Clarification of P.L. 94-142 for the Classroom Teacher, published by Research for Better Schools, Inc., Philadelphia, Pa., 1978, p. 17. Reprinted by permission.

A fourth grader returns from school one afternoon, behaving unusually quietly. Later that evening the child, who is somewhat of a worrier, bursts into tears; she tells her parents that the teacher set up new reading groups that day, and that she got put in the "retarded" group. Her parents ask her why she believes that and find out that one of the mainstreamed students has been placed in her group. The next day, the mother calls the principal to voice her concern.

How do you suppose the child and her parents are feeling? How might the mother behave on the telephone? How can the principal express concern, yet defend mainstreaming practices? Should the teacher have behaved differently? What are some possible reasons for grouping normal and handicapped children for instructional purposes?

Role-Play

Enact the telephone conversation between the principal and the parent. Then enact the principal's subsequent discussion with the classroom teacher.

Evaluate both role-plays. How can classroom teachers make the principal's position easier in assuring compliance with 94-142? How can teachers and principals ensure good home-school communication regarding implementation of the law?

Planning an In-service Day

Teachers who work with handicapped children typically interact with numerous other professionals. They work with speech and language therapists, physical and occupational therapists, school psychologists, psychiatrists, social workers, and so on.

Often teachers are able to make suggestions for and plan their own in-service days. Consider planning an in-service day for the purpose of enhancing communication among professionals working with the handicapped children in your school. Outline the content of the day's program, list the participants, and describe the nature of the activities.

Identifying Support Service Personnel in Your Local School District

An important component of the IEP is the identification of support services needed by the student. Teachers, then, should be aware of local professionals who provide these services. Many of these persons, such as guidance counselors, may be directly employed by your local school district. Others, such as a physical therapist, may not, and the school must purchase that person's services.

List the names and professional addresses of persons in your area who are available to provide special kinds of support services. Are any kinds of services unavailable in your area? You can answer this question by considering all types of handicapping conditions and the kinds of support personnel they might require.

Critical Incidents to Consider

Three critical incidents involving working with other professionals are reprinted on the following pages. They present realistic situations for you to respond to, and you can "think through" your reactions and feelings to these problem situations. You should react spontaneously—keep your answers brief and to the point. Your written reactions should be a true reflection of what you really would do if you were in the situation. After responding to all three incidents, look back over your reactions. How satisfied are you with your reactions? Now that you think again about the situation, would you handle it differently? How?

Getting Coworkers to Cooperate

You are a high school learning disabilities specialist. This is your second
year in this school and you have been experiencing reasonable success with
your students. You are receiving more and more referrals from certain teachers, though. Additionally, teachers seem to be sending you children who have
behavior rather than learning problems. You have always accepted these referrals, trying to establish a cooperative atmosphere.

Now you go to one of these teachers to ask if he will accept one of your slow
learners in his biology class. He flatly refuses, saying that he is too busy
to give individual help to that child.

What Are My Reactions and Feelings?

1. I would remind him of _____

    _____.

2. I would meet with the other teachers, saying _____

    _____.

3. When I received new referrals, I would _____

    _____.

4. I would meet with the principal and recommend _____

    _____.

5. I would try to _____

    _____.

6. Other. _____

    _____.

Source: From Exceptional Previews, A Self-Evaluation Handbook For Special Education Students by Carol A. Cartwright and Sara J. Forsberg. © 1979 by Wadsworth Publishing Company, Inc., Belmont, California 94002. Reprinted by permission of the publisher.

Coping with Hostility from Coworkers

Your self-contained class for multiply handicapped children is housed, along with two others, at one end of an elementary school. Because of the special needs of your children, you three teachers are not assigned to bus duty, recess duty, or school program responsibilities. As you three walk in, slightly late, to a teachers' meeting, you overhear a group of teachers talking about you. "They really·have it easy, you know. . . ." You feel they are envious because you have few children and school duties.

What Are My Reactions and Feelings?

1. I would pretend not to have heard the comments and _____

    _____ .

2. I would show that I had heard their talk by _____

    _____ .

3. I would confront them, saying _____

    _____ .

4. I would try to _____

    _____ .

5. I would discuss this problem with _____

    _____ .

6. I would avoid these teachers as much as possible, and when I was with them

    _____

    _____ .

7. Other. _____

    _____ .

Source: From _Exceptional Previews, A Self-Evaluation Handbook For Special Education Students_ by Carol A. Cartwright and Sara J. Forsberg. © 1979 by Wadsworth Publishing Company, Inc., Belmont, California 94002. Reprinted by permission of the publisher.

Planning an In-Service Program

You are coordinating the mainstreaming program in a middle grade elementary unit. In addition, you do special programming in a resource room for approximately twenty children. The elementary supervisor has asked you to do an in-service workshop for the teachers in your unit. Although you welcome the opportunity and know that several teachers could benefit from such a workshop, you don't want it to interfere with the rapport you've developed with these teachers. They now view you as a peer, rather than as a supervisor.

What Are My Reactions and Feelings?

1. I would prefer to find another person because _____

    _____.

2. I would do it myself since _____

    _____.

3. If I had to be the person responsible for the workshop, I would

    a. try to seem less authoritarian by _____

        _____.

    b. try to make the workshop meaningful for the staff by _____

        _____.

4. Other. _____

    _____.

Source: From Exceptional Previews, A Self-Evaluation Handbook For Special Education Students by Carol A. Cartwright and Sara J. Forsberg. © 1979 by Wadsworth Publishing Company, Inc., Belmont, California 94002. Reprinted by permission of the publisher.

Section H: Working With Parents

Put Yourself in Their Shoes

Those who have considered carefully the problems facing parents of exceptional children report that, all too often, parents must deal with members of the "helping professions" who do not help. Take some time to read the article, "Let Us All Stop Blaming the Parents," which is reprinted on the following pages.* Let it be an opportunity for you to bring out and examine your personal feelings about working with the parents of exceptional children. After reading the article and reflecting on your feelings, make a list of at least five new insights you have gained about yourself and about your feelings and reactions toward the parents of exceptional children.

*Reprinted with permission of The Exceptional Parent magazine. Copyright © 1971, Psy-ed Corporation, 296 Boylston Street, Boston, Massachusetts 02116.

Let Us All Stop Blaming The Parents

"I'm sick and tired of being blamed for my child's problems! You guys are all alike. You ask us a lot of questions, make the child go through a lot of tests and then tell us that you can do nothing. If we complain, you say that if we cannot accept the limitations of the child, we'll only increase his problems. Why don't you do something, anything?"

How often have you felt like saying this, but stifled the wish because you were afraid you would be labeled a "trouble-maker"; and then, no one would help you?

Occasionally, the professional encourages you to express all of your feelings. He explains that it is really not your fault that there is so little knowledge or so few resources available to help children that have such a disability. He tells you that it is quite common to feel angry when you are in a situation where so little can be done and when you feel that you are at the mercy of professionals. His words can be comforting, but this message is more compli-cated than it first appears. On the one hand, he is telling you that it is all right to be angry. At the same time, he is making it clear that the profes-sional agency should not be the target.

It is also true that merely expressing feelings is not always helpful. What can you do with these feelings if you cannot attach them to something and/or do something constructive? When people can do nothing to participate actively in the solution of their problems, they usually attach these feelings to them-selves. If others can justify their inability to work with you, who else can you attack but yourself when nothing seems to help? Ultimately, you are left with the feeling that because you produced the child, you are to blame for the problems. After all, there would be no problems if there was no child.

This process, by which parents and experts mutually conclude that the major responsibility for failure of programs resides within the parents, is care-fully examined by William Ryan in his recent book, Blaming The Victim (New York: Pantheon, 1971).

He illustrates how, unaware of society's role, the client and professional scrutinize and attack each other when programs fail. He makes it clear that any problem and its solution is shaped by what takes place in society. For example, in the society that prizes and rewards youth and energy, "old" peo-ple become a problem. In this society, resources are expended on helping people remain young. Unless society's attitudes toward aging are changed, problems of adequate health care, appropriate housing, and full opportunities for older people to feel useful may never be addressed. He points out that society, in limiting resources that are available, victimizes both client and professional. This part of their mutual problem can only be solved if they join together in their demands for a reallocation of priorities.

An examination of the typical situations that families with a disabled child encounter will illustrate how Dr. Ryan's thesis can be applied to "exceptional parents."

Let us look at the family when they first decide they need a professional judgment about the child's difficulty. It is customary for the expert to take a family history. He usually asks when the family first observed the child having problems, what life with the child was like before they recognized the problem, about their current activities with the youngster, and what finally made them seek help.

Implicitly, the very act of history gathering, so vital to any diagnostic assessment, contributes to locating the blame in the parent. Both professional and parent assume that the family's current program is inadequate. If this was not so, they would not need help. They further assume that if the family had been able to come sooner, their inadequate program would have begun to be altered. These two assumptions lead both to focus on the family's life and attitudes, thereby reinforcing the feeling that the parent is at fault.

Let us take a broader view of this situation. With many disabilities, it is clear at birth that life for both family and infant will be difficult. Often the hospital staff does not clearly explain to the family what they are likely to encounter. Nor do they make it clear why it will be necessary for them to initiate and maintain contact with a variety of specialists. They seldom take the responsibility for calling these families after they leave the hospital to find out what has happened or how the child is doing. Until society makes sure that there are adequate assessments and services for all babies and their parents, the problems of early diagnosis and appropriate intervention will persist.

Let us now consider the disabled child when he reaches school age. There may be many problems in providing an adequate education. The family discusses this with their elementary school principal. The principal carefully describes his lengthy efforts to include disabled children in school, either in regular or special class programs. He then points out that all these efforts have failed for children with your child's disability; and that, in fact, many of these children have suffered so much from the school experience, it would have been better for them if they had not attended at all.

Here, the parents are encouraged to accept, not only the assumption that the reason for a lack of educational opportunities lies in the child's disability, but also that their desire to have the child included in public school is part of the child's problem. Once again, they are asked to assume blame for their own activities.

Another possibility is that the school dilemma exists because schools do not have enough experience with children with disabilities. Further, they will never gain this experience unless the school system provides either the resources or money necessary to develop programs for all children with disabilities. In addition, society is not living up to its own mandate that all children have equal rights to educational opportunities.

Failing to find an appropriate public school placement, the family finds a special program for their child. The child has just finished his third year. The family has been called in by the school director to discuss their child's progress. The director tells the family that the child cannot return in the fall. There has been so little progress during the course of the past year that it is not worth the family's money or the school's time to continue the child in this program. The parent is asked to accept the twofold assumption that continuous progress is necessary every year and the lack of it is part of their child's disability.

An alternate view is that the school's expectation of progress may be unrealistic. So little is known about the natural progress of children with disabilities through the course of their development, an adequate judgment about appropriate school progress may not be possible. Further, until society provides a reasonable alternative, this school may still be the most profitable place for the child to be.

Another familiar problem for parents is finding constructive recreational activities for the disabled child. Parents, concerned about the lack of activity in the child's life, go to the special class teacher. They ask her to increase the child's time at school and/or suggest what they can do for him at home or in the community. She reminds them that the child had attended school for full days previously. Supposedly, this was too much for him. Three days a week was found to be more appropriate. She also reminds them that a year ago when they increased his activities at home this had not worked. Again, the parents are asked to locate the reason for the restricted program in the child and themselves.

An alternative is that the school does not have sufficient flexibility to create a better program. In addition, although the family has difficulties with the child, they also have broad experience and understanding of him. This understanding must be utilized if anyone wants to enrich the child's life either at home or in school. Further, the problem also exists because society has not ensured that all of its programs be available to disabled children.

More successful programs of treatment for the disabled child are being developed. Because they usually have limited space, they carefully scrutinize all new applicants. The family of a disabled child, hearing reports of success in a new treatment program, apply in behalf of their child. They tell the director that they are not happy with the child's current treatment agency because it does not seem to be an appropriate place for their youngster.

The family's and child's experience with this program is carefully reviewed. Then the director tells them that his agency has a long waiting list and is unlikely to have space for their child. The director often assumes that these are critical parents and are unlikely to cooperate with any program. The family is encouraged to remain with their own treatment agency. He tells them that their challenge is to learn how they might help the child make better use of the current program.

Here, the parent cannot even confront the assumption that their inability to come to peace with their own treatment agency is an index of their ability to work with any other agency. The family is also expected to accept the premise that no program can truly meet the needs of their disabled child.

A broader view is that their current treatment program has very special weaknesses. Further, parents can adequately assess what contributes to their child's progress. It might be more constructive if society asked why it expends so much energy encouraging parents to accept less than the best for their children.

Families with children with disabilities and specialists who serve them will always have special problems in constructing adequate programs. They must continuously evaluate their mutual activities in order to improve their ability to provide a better life for the child. However, parents and professionals also must have available financial resources and community support if they are to fully expand opportunities for all disabled children. Otherwise, both parents and professionals will travel in a continuous circle; neither having enough experience to plan new programs—and without new programs they can never have the necessary experience.

In the current situation, with limited facilities, the professional selects those families and children most likely to benefit from existing programs. This means that the majority of children with disabilities have minimal support. The family must then examine what they or the child must have or must be able to do to make themselves acceptable for agency service. They often find themselves trying new things, whether they are suitable or not in order to cross the agency threshold. Trapped in this fruitless and, often painful, mutual encounter, family and agency unnecessarily expend a great deal of energy criticizing each other. Until they join forces and also demand that society make more available, they will be limited in providing new and better opportunities for the disabled.

In considering who changes society, some have divided the world into three groups of people. There are those who can tolerate the everyday stresses and strains of life; they say little, and these are the average people. There are those who cannot tolerate the everyday stresses and strains of life; and they shout, and these are our leaders. Then, there are those who cannot tolerate the stresses and strains of life; and they whisper, and these are our victims. Society has generally demanded that families of disabled children whisper. Society has implicitly blamed and punished those parents and professionals who have attempted to shout about their pain and anguish. And finally, professionals and families have often, unwittingly, accepted society's limited investment in them.

We do not believe that the parents or the professionals should stop their search for better ways of helping the disabled child within the current context. We do believe that without dreams of the ideal, they may wander aimlessly, searching for new directions.

We are reminded of one of Robert Kennedy's favorite quotations: "Some men see things as they are and say, why. I dream of things that never were and say, why not."

Critiquing Popular Press Material

Many parents of handicapped children report that their parenting responsibilities are especially difficult because even the usual support systems (e.g., conversations with neighbors, and magazine articles and books on child rearing) do not apply.

1. Visit a local bookstore or library. Choose several of the more popular books published for parents, such as <u>Between Parent and Child</u> by H. Ginott. Assume the role of the parent of a handicapped child. Write out a paragraph describing your child—age, sex, handicapping condition, any special management or learning problems. Critique the books you've chosen according to how useful they are to you. You might consider questions such as:

> *Does the book focus at all on parenting tips for those who have handicapped children?
> *Is the generic material in the book applicable to parents of handicapped children?
> *Does the content have a positive, negative, or neutral approach toward handicapped children?
> *Does the book attempt to attribute causality to handicapping conditions?
> *How accurate is the information related to handicapped children?
> *How might this book be made more appropriate?

2. Read several articles dealing with handicapped children in popular magazines. Critique them in terms of accuracy of content, appropriateness and specificity of advice, humanistic treatment of the handicapped.

Assessing Your Reactions Toward Parents

The following instrument has been developed to help teachers focus on specific aspects of their relationships with parents.* The authors suggest that you mark your reactions with U for "usually," S for "seldom," and N for "never." You might use the questionnaire at various times (e.g., beginning, middle, and end of year); or, for comparison, you might have others rate you.

After you have filled out the instrument, discuss your reactions with other group members. What do you consider appropriate reactions? Does research support your positions?

*In R. L. Kroth, and R. L. Simpson, <u>Parent Conferences as a Teaching Strategy</u> (Denver, Colo.: Love Publishing, 1977), pp. 14-16. Reprinted by permission.

Are You a Teacher Who . . .

A	B	C	
			1. never admits to a parent that you're wrong?
			2. has a sense of humor in a conference?
			3. lets parents smoke in a conference?
			4. serves coffee to parents during a conference?
			5. doesn't have any favorites?
			6. shows expression and emotions in a conference?
			7. shows expression and emotions in parent groups?
			8. starts conferences or parent meetings on time?
			9. has contacts with parents?
			10. stops parent meetings at a scheduled time?
			11. has conferences in parents' homes?
			12. compares students with their older siblings?
			13. finds it hard to say "I don't know" to parents?
			14. talks less than 50% of each conference?
			15. talks about your own problems and solutions in conferences?
			16. sits behind a desk during conferences?
			17. enjoys parent conferences?
			18. has examples of children's work to show parents?
			19. calls parents when things go well with their child?
			20. sends notes home when children have behavioral problems?
			21. uses grades to keep students in line?
			22. has ever had a principal sit in on one of your conferences?

A	B	C

23. finds yourself criticizing more than praising your parents?

24. has ever had dinner at a student's home?

25. has ever had a parent over for dinner or a meeting at your home?

26. feels that parents have lost the respect of their children?

27. feels that parents have lost control of their children?

28. finds yourself physically drained at the end of a series of conferences?

29. has parent group meetings?

30. has strong negative feelings about certain racial or sexual groups?

31. prefers to have conferences with fathers rather than mothers?

32. studies a child's folder and past achievements before a conference?

33. argues with parents?

34. feels intimidated by parents?

35. demonstrates to parents effective ways to work with their child?

36. likes to problem-solve with parents?

37. involves parents in planning for their child?

38. encourages parents to visit class during class sessions?

39. uses parents as aides in the class?

40. does not want parents to teach their own children?

41. is honest with parents?

42. listens to parents?

43. dreads conference time?

A	B	C

44. has parents call on the telephone to your home in the evening?

45. is positively reinforcing?

46. sends home daily report cards?

47. prepares handbooks or handouts for parents?

48. has good attendance at conference time or for group meetings?

49. has students sit in on conferences with their parents?

50. talks about other teachers to parents?

Planning and Recording Parent Conferences

It is important for teachers of exceptional children to be skilled in conducting parent conferences. In those conferences teachers must often provide emotional support to parents, assist parents in parent-child interaction, provide an informational link between home and school.

In this activity you are asked to role-play a parent-teacher conference, following the guidelines provided. Take time to plan well. Decide on the nature of the child's problem, the teacher's objectives, the parents' interaction patterns and concerns. At the end of the conference the "teacher" should fill out the recording sheet on the next page. As the group evaluates your conference, check to see if the "parents" agree with the data recorded by the "teacher" on the recording form. If disagreement exists, discuss how it could be remedied.

Guidelines for the Conference

1.   Prepare adequately—gather any child materials or data you will be using, write down your objectives for the meeting, write out any questions you want to ask, make certain that parents will be physically and emotionally comfortable.

2.   Conduct conference adequately—begin with positive comments about the child, listen to parents' questions and concerns, present your information and questions smoothly and clearly, take as few obvious notes as possible.

3.   Summarize—end with a summary of decisions made, questions unanswered, arrangements for follow-up, and optimistic message where possible.

Parent-Teacher Conference

Name _____

Date _____

1. Relevant Information

   a. Developmental History

   b. School History

   c. Sociological Information

   d. Other

2.

Objectives of Meeting	Accomplished?

3.

Decisions Made	Person Responsible	Follow-up Arrangements	Done

Writing Progress Reports

In many school districts, teachers do not regularly send home written progress reports. Teachers who work with exceptional children often must do this, however, since the standard report card forms are inadequate reports of children's developmental levels and progress.

Good progress reports have many of these characteristics:

1.   They follow a clear structure so they can be easily read; side headings (e.g., Language Arts, Arithmetic) are used to emphasize the structure.

2.   They are written frequently enough to report progress as it happens, rather than months later.

3.   They serve as reinforcers to parents. That is, teachers report on progress in areas where parents as well as teachers are working.

4.   They are written at a level of communication appropriate for the recipient.

5.   They are useful to parents. That is, they give parents specific information as to where the child is functioning and how they can encourage the child to perform certain tasks.

Assignment

Write a progress report for a child you have observed, or for a hypothetical child. Your information, too, may be hypothetical. Try to follow the guidelines carefully; however, you will need to construct your own outline based on grade level and behavior characteristics of the child.

Which aspects of the report were easiest? Most difficult for you? How might you improve these skills?

Explaining the Concept of Least Restrictive Environment

Mainstreaming is probably a new concept to the parents of normal children. Many of them fear that all kinds of handicapped children will now be placed in their child's classroom. How will you explain the concept of placement within the least restrictive environment? Outline your presentation, using local types of educational placements as examples of progressions from restrictive to least restrictive educational settings.

Part Three:

Resources

Introduction to Part Three

Often the key to helping handicapped children and their families is for the right person to have the right information at the right time. Obviously, no one can know all there is to know about working with exceptional youngsters. The information explosion is as much a fact in special education as it is in other fields. Even though you do not have the information yourself, however, you ought to be able to locate it and be able to do so quickly while the need is urgent and the time is ripe for real use of the information. That's where we come in. The purpose of Part Three is to alert you to what is available in the field of special education. We have included both print and nonprint resources that can be used by different audiences. These resources should help you find information for yourself as you teach and work with exceptional children; for colleagues who are seeking information about the exceptional children in their care; for parents, community leaders, and the general public; and for nonhandicapped children in schools everywhere.

Part Three begins with a comprehensive list of manufacturers, distributors, and publishers of special education equipment and materials. Companies who have collections of special education materials in addition to their general education materials, and companies who specialize in materials for the handicapped are included. A list of organizations and advocacy groups that work on behalf of special disability groups, as well as the exceptional in general, is given next. Lists of films and other media, and books for parents, teachers, and children round out Part Three. In all cases, we worked hard to be accurate so you can find what you need, write to companies, contact local chapters of organizations, and so on. Listing the information does not constitute an endorsement—your needs and the number and variability of the information available precludes that.

Manufacturers, Distributors, and Publishers of Special Education Equipment and Materials

Abt Books
> 55 Wheeler Street
> Cambridge, MA 02138
> Resource books for parents and teachers of the handicapped.

Academic Therapy Publications
> London Bridge
> Suite D, 7901 Brookford Circle
> Baltimore, MD 21208
> Special education materials, including language arts, mathematics, teaching aids and remedial aids, secondary education, vocational education, and professional books.

Adapt Press, Inc.
> 808 West Avenue North
> Sioux Falls, SD 57104
> Professional books for teachers of preschool, kindergarten, and special education classes.

Agency for Instructional Television
> Box A
> Bloomington, IN 47401
> Large selection of films and video cassettes; preschool through adult.

Allyn and Bacon, Inc.
> College Division, Department 894
> 470 Atlantic Avenue
> Boston, MA 02210
> Special education textbooks, language arts textbooks, elementary education textbooks.

American Association for the Advancement of Science
> 1515 Massachusetts Avenue, N.W.
> Washington, DC 20005
> Science Education News

American Federation of Teachers, AFL-CIO
> 11 Dupont Circle N.W.
> Washington, DC 20036
> Selected publications for special education.

American Foundation for the Blind
>   Consumer Products Department
>   15 West 16th Street
>   New York, NY 10011
>   Products for people with vision problems; publications, research reports, films for and about the visually handicapped.

American Guidance Service
>   Publishers' Building
>   Circle Pines, MN 55014
>   Tests—ability and aptitude, achievement, and diagnostic, maturity and readiness, speech; instructional programs; educational materials.

American Printing House for the Blind
>   1839 Frankfort Avenue
>   Louisville, KY 40206
>   A variety of materials for and about the visually handicapped.

American Science & Engineering, Inc.
>   20 Overland Street
>   Boston, MA 02215
>   Attn: Education Division
>   Early childhood curriculum—a preschool and kindergarten program designed to foster the development of logical thinking processes and associated language; based on the research of Jean Piaget.

Angeles Nursery Toys
>   4105 North Fairfax Avenue
>   Arlington, VA 22203
>   Wheeltoys.

Argus Communications
>   7440 Natchez Avenue
>   Niles, IL 60648
>   Materials for the curriculum areas of: language arts/English, mathematics, social studies, career education, family living, art/humanities, bilingual education, special education, guidance/counseling, values education, and teacher training/in-service; grade 1 through adult.

Aspen Systems Corporation
>   20010 Century Boulevard
>   Germantown, MD 20767
>   Texts for special education.

Audio Visual Products Division
>   7100 McCormick Road
>   Chicago, IL 60645
>   The Language Master System—instructional devices and programs for all curriculum areas; preschool through grade 12.

AVKO
    Educational Research Foundation, Inc.
    3084 West Willard Road
    Birch Run, MI   48415
    Language arts materials for children with special needs.

The Barber Center Press, Inc.
    136 East Avenue
    Erie, PA   16507
    Materials for vocational/career training, assessment devices for community living, and sheltered work experiences for mentally retarded adults and teenagers.

Barr Films
    3490 East Foothill Boulevard
    Pasadena, CA   91107
    Films for use in all subject areas; kindergarten through adult.

Behavior Systems, Inc.
    P.O. Box 19045
    Kansas City, MO   64141
    "Five Steps to Better Child Behavior"—cassette program for parents.

Benchmark Films, Inc.
    145 Scarborough Road
    Briarcliff Manor, NY   10510
    16 mm and 8 mm films; elementary through adult levels. Subject areas: drug abuse, ecology, filmmaking, health and psychology, home economics and consumer education, human reproduction, humanities and art, language arts, social sciences, natural science, world history.

BFA Educational Media
    2211 Michigan Avenue
    Santa Monica, CA   90404
    Super 8 silent film loops, filmstrips, book/record sets, multimedia kits, and study prints for all curriculum areas; elementary level.

Book-Lab, Inc.
    1449 37th Street
    Brooklyn, NY   11218
    Activity and idea books for prereading and reading, science, and math for special needs children; materials for establishing a peer-tutor program.

Bowmar/Noble
    4563 Colorado Boulevard
    Los Angeles, CA   90039
    Early childhood programs for language arts, reading, social studies, science, music, and perceptual-motor development.

Campus Film Distributors Corp.
  14 Madison Avenue
  P.O. Box 206
  Valhalla, NY 10595
  Wide variety of films for early childhood and special education.

Carousel Films, Inc.
  1501 Broadway, Suite 1503
  New York, NY 10036
  16 mm and Super 8 mm films on a wide variety of topics; elementary
  through adult levels.

C. C. Publications, Inc.
  P.O. Box 23699
  Tigard, OR 97223
  Materials for speech/language disordered; learning disabled, EMR/TMR;
  deaf/hard of hearing; bilingual, and early childhood education.

The Chapel Hill Training—Outreach Project
  Lincoln Center
  Chapel Hill, NC 27514
  Anne R. Sanford, Director
  Publications: Working With Families: A Manual for Development Centers;
  Learning Accomplishment Profile; A Manual for Use of the Learning Ac-
  complishment Profile; A Model for Resource Services to the Young Handi-
  capped Child in a Public School Setting; The Chapel Hill Model for
  Training Head Start Personnel in Mainstreaming Handicapped Children.

Cheviot Corp.
  Department M641
  Box 34485
  Los Angeles, CA 90034
  Distributors of Rhythms Productions Records; selection of records for
  basic rhythmic activities, folk dance, modern dance, and recorders.

Childcraft Education Corp.
  20 Kilmer Road
  Edison, NJ 08817
  Complete line of classroom materials for preschool and primary grades;
  includes storage and display units, furniture, classroom aids, active
  play materials, dramatic play, creative expression, books, beginning
  skills and concepts, basic primary skills, and infant equipment and toys.

Childhood Resources, Inc.
  5307 Lee Highway
  Arlington, VA 22207
  Early childhood education tape cassette programs; Tindell's and Angeles
  wheeled toys; audiovisual library for the early childhood educator;

audiovisual programs on community services, living and learning with the handicapped child, and infant development.

Churchill Films
        662 North Robertson Boulevard
        Los Angeles, CA 90069
        Films for language arts, social studies, science, health and safety, personal guidance, career guidance, the arts, teacher education, and foreign languages.

Clearvue, Inc.
        6666 North Oliphant Avenue
        Chicago, IL 60631
        Materials, texts, and programs in language arts, basic concepts, social studies, science, guidance, health, metric system, handicrafts; kindergarten through secondary.

Closer Look
        Box 1492
        Washington, DC 20013
        National resource center for parents (and professionals who work with parents) of handicapped children.

Cognitive Developmental Designs, Inc.
        P.O. Box 310
        Back Bay Annex
        Boston, MA 02117
        Materials and films for special education.

Community Playthings
        Rifton, NY 12471
        Early childhood materials including furniture, blocks, large muscle play equipment, manipulative toys, housekeeping and dramatic play equipment, transportation toys, and books and records.

Constructive Playthings
        1040 East 85th Street
        Kansas City, MO 64131
        Complete line of playground equipment, educational materials, toys, classroom furniture, and books; preschool through intermediate grades and special education.

Consulting Psychologists Press, Inc.
        577 College Avenue
        Palo Alto, CA 94306
        Diagnostic tests and teaching materials for special education; preschool to secondary/adult.

The Continental Press, Inc.
    Elizabethtown, PA 17022
    or
    2336 Farrington Street
    Dallas, TX 75207
    or
    P.O. Box 554
    Elgin, IL 60120
    or
    127 International Boulevard, N.W.
    Atlanta, GA 30303
    or
    407 S.W. 11th Avenue
    Portland, OR 97205
    or
    c/o Vroman's
    2085 East Foothill Boulevard
    Pasadena, CA 91109
    Special education kits and series covering a variety of topics.

Council for Exceptional Children
    1920 Association Drive
    Reston, VA 22091
    An extensive collection of print materials and media on a variety of
    special education topics ranging from policy analysis to teaching tips.

Creative Curriculum, Inc.
    15681 Commerce Lane
    Huntington Beach, CA 92649
    Reading programs, perceptual training, and study skills materials for
    kindergarten through adult levels.

Creative Playthings
    P.O. Box 1100
    Princeton, NJ 08540
    Toys for children ages 3 months to 10 years.

CRM McGraw-Hill Films
    110 15th Street
    Del Mar, CA 92014
    16 mm films with instructor's guides on: developmental psychology,
    teaching techniques, special education; behavior modification, and
    special education; mainstreaming.

Cuisenaire Company of America, Inc.
    12 Church Street
    New Rochelle, NY 10805
    Mathematical models, books, and enrichment materials; elementary level.

Curriculum Associates
       6 Henshaw Street
       Woburn, MA 01801
       Instructional materials for reading, composition, spelling, vocabulary,
       grammar and mechanics, research and study skills, and arithmetic skills;
       teacher resource materials; grades K-12.

Danmar Products, Inc.
       2390 Winewood
       Ann Arbor, MI 48103
       Headgear for special needs.

Day Care and Child Development Council of America, Inc.
       1012 14th Street, N.W.
       11th Floor
       Washington, DC 20005
       Publishes a variety of materials dealing with day care and early child-
       hood education.

T. D. Denison & Co., Inc.
       5100 West 82nd Street
       Minneapolis, MN 55437
       Books and teaching aids for all grade levels; professional books.

Developmental Learning Materials
       7440 Natchez Avenue
       Niles, IL 60648
       Materials on self-concept, motor skills, visual perception, auditory
       perception, language, reading, handwriting, social awareness, careers,
       mathematics, reference materials and teaching aids.

DORMAC, Inc.
       P.O. Box 752
       Beaverton, OR 97005
       Educational materials for the hearing impaired.

Doubleday Multimedia
       P.O. Box 11607
       Santa Ana, CA 92705
       16 mm films for language arts, science, social studies, mathematics,
       and career and vocational education; grades K-12.

EAST, Inc.
       P.O. Box 13375
       University Station
       Gainesville, FL 32604
       Instructional materials and games for preschool through grade 12.

EDITS
>P.O. Box 7234
>San Diego, CA 92107
>Individualized mathematics program including assessment tests; grades K-12.

Edmark Associates
>P.O. Box 3903
>Bellevue, WA 98009
>Special education materials, texts, reading programs, assessment tools.

Education Achievement Corp.
>P.O. Box 7310
>Waco, TX 76710
>Multimedia career education program; grades K-8.

Education for Special Needs
>85 Main Street
>Watertown, MA 02172
>Teaching and in-service training materials for special educators.

Educational Activities, Inc.
>P.O. Box 392
>Freeport, NY 11520
>Records, cassettes, filmstrips, and kits for the areas of: adult basic education, career awareness, consumer education, driver education, early childhood, guidance, learning disabilities, special education, language arts, science, social studies, mathematics, music.

Educational Aids
>Hampton Richey
>845 Wisteria Drive
>Fremont, CA 94538
>Phonics materials, music materials, children's creative play songs and records, square dance records, books, math materials.

Educational Design, Inc.
>47 West 13 Street
>New York, NY 10011
>Texts and materials in life skills (math, reading), job attitudes and habits, social studies.

Educational Development Center
>15 Miflin Place
>Cambridge, MA 02138
>Programs to train parents and teachers.

Educational Products, Inc.
>5005 West 110th Street
>Oak Lawn, IL 60453
>Bold Beginning in Early Learning—36-week sequential developmental curriculum.

Educational Progress Corporation
>P.O. Box 45663
>Tulsa, OK 74145
>Texts and materials in all subject areas for grades K-secondary.

Educational Reading Services
>320 Route 17
>Mahwah, NJ 07430
>Basic resource materials for teaching reading; grades K-8; educational relations.

Educational Service, Inc.
>Box 219
>Stevensville, MI 49127
>Idea and duplicator books covering a wide variety of topics and age ranges.

Educational Teaching Aids
>159 West Kinzie Street
>Chicago, IL 60610
>Materials for the areas of mathematics, language arts, early childhood, and special education.

EMC Corporation
>180 East Sixth Street
>St. Paul, MN 55101
>Special education materials including career education/guidance, vocational education, special needs; K-secondary.

Encyclopedia Britannica
>Educational Corporation
>425 North Michigan Avenue
>Chicago, IL 60611
>Multimedia programs to help develop basic skills in young children; filmstrips, 8 mm films, kits, books, study prints, recordings, transparencies in the areas of language arts, the arts, foreign language, social studies, science, mathematics, bilingual education, career education, health, physical education, special education, and early childhood education; grades K-12.

ERIC/ECE Newsletter
>   Publications Office
>   College of Education
>   University of Illinois
>   805 West Pennsylvania Avenue
>   Urbana, IL 61801
>   News items on all aspects of early childhood education; annotated
>   listings of recent publications and ERIC documents.

Exceptional Child Development Center, Inc.
>   755 Liberty Avenue
>   Pittsburgh, PA 15222
>   Distributors of: The Exceptional Line
>   P.O. Box 976
>   Braintree, MA 02184
>   Toys, games, and play equipment for toddlers to 12-year-olds;
>   selection of items for special education.

The Exceptional Parent Press
>   Room 708 Statler Office Building
>   Boston, MA 02116
>   Publishers of The Exceptional Parent magazine and books for parents
>   and teachers of exceptional children.

Exceptional Play
>   P.O. Box 1015
>   Lawrence, KS 66044
>   Custom designed playground equipment; variety of play materials that
>   are adaptable to different skill levels and useful in a variety of
>   developmental settings.

Fawcett Publications, Inc.
>   Fawcett Place
>   Greenwich, CT 06830
>   Paperback books.

Fearon Publishers
>   6 Davis Drive
>   Belmont, CA 94002
>   Resource books for teachers on: arts and crafts, bulletin boards,
>   classroom activities, general interest, language arts, mathematics,
>   physical education, science.

Film Incorporated
>   Department S.
>   1144 Wilmette Avenue
>   Wilmette, IL 60091
>   Movie strips, script readers, and reading skills kits made from movies
>   of well-known children's books.

Flaghouse, Inc.
>   18 West 18th Street
>   New York, NY 10011
>   Motor activity equipment for special populations; includes motor develop-
>   ment, socialization, body image, physical education, and recreation.

Follett Publishing Co.
>   1010 West Washington Boulevard
>   Chicago, IL 60607
>   Publishes assessment materials, instructional materials, and profession-
>   al books on early childhood education.

Gallaudet College Press
>   Washington, DC
>   Teaching aids of the Signed English System.

Games Central, c/o Abt Associates
>   55 Wheeler Street
>   Cambridge, MA 02138
>   Instructional kits for the areas of language arts, mathematics, science,
>   and social studies; grades K-12; books for teachers.

General Learning Corp.
>   Morristown, NJ 07960
>   Language arts games; elementary level.

General Secretariat
Organization of American States
>   Department of Publications
>   Washington, DC 20006
>   OAS Catalog of Publications—offers a wide variety of publications on
>   Latin America that are useful to teachers and students.

Golden Press—Educational Division
>   Western Publishing Company, Inc.
>   150 Parish Drive
>   Wayne, NJ 07470
>   Curriculum-related books and audio materials preschool through secondary.

Goodyear Publishing Co.
>   P.O. Box 486
>   Pacific Palisades, CA 90272
>   Activity books for language arts, social studies, value clarification,
>   affective education, science, and learning centers; professional books
>   on general methods, open education, early childhood education, testing
>   and counseling, and educational issues.

Grune & Stratton, Inc.
    111 Fifth Avenue
    New York, NY 10003
    Textbooks and testing materials for special education, speech and hear-
    ing, psychological testing and psychology, and child psychology.

Gryphon House
    3706 Otis House
    P.O. Box 217
    Mt. Rainier, MD 20822
    Books for young children with special emphasis on books with nonsexist,
    multiethnic content; materials include books about special children
    and resource books for teachers.

Harper & Row Publishers, Inc.
    School Department
    2500 Crawford Avenue
    Evanston, IL 60201
    Textbook series for all curriculum areas; preschool through grade 12.

Harvest Educational Labs
    73 Pelham Street
    Newport, RI 02840
    Special education texts, materials, films, survival skills (secondary
    education).

Hawkins & Associates, Inc.
    804 D Street, N.E.
    Washington, DC 20002
    Materials for the fields of leisure, special education, career education,
    rehabilitation, physical education, geriatrics, travel-tourism, camping,
    and environmental education.

Hayes Books Inc.
    4235 South Memorial Drive
    Tulsa, OK 74145
    Discovery books for elementary and secondary grade children.

D.C. Heath & Co.
    125 Spring Street
    Lexington, MA 02173
    EDGE 1—Multimedia program that provides learning experiences in oral
    development, auditory perception, visual discrimination, reading skills,
    number concepts, form recognition, eye-hand coordination, physical
    adeptness, and social interaction; preschool through grade 2.

High Interest Teaching Systems
> P.O. Box 727
> San Juan Capistrano, CA 92675
> Primary Reading Program—includes diagnosis and placement, song charts, songs, skill sheets, workbooks, manipulative games.

Highlights for Children
> 2300 West Fifth Avenue
> Columbus, OH 43272
> Activity books and instructional materials; preschool and elementary levels.

High/Scope Educational Research Foundation
> 600 North River Street
> Ypsilanti, MI 48197
> Audiovisual materials and books for preschool and elementary teachers.

J. R. Holcomb Company
> Educational Materials
> 3000 Quigley Road
> Cleveland, OH 44113
> Competency-based curriculum for junior-senior high schools, adult, and special education.

Holt, Rinehart and Winston
> 383 Madison Avenue
> New York, NY 10017
> Psychology and educational textbooks.

Houghton Mifflin
> Editorial and International Departments
> One Beacon Street
> Boston, MA 02107
> Regional Sales Office: Pennington-Hopewell Road
> Hopewell, NJ 08525
> Textbooks on foundations of education, educational evaluation, elementary curriculum methods, secondary curriculum methods, administration and supervision, special education, counseling and guidance. Mathematics materials including Individual Pupil Monitoring System, School Mathematics Concepts and Skills series, metric products, and other materials.

Hubbard
> P.O. Box 104
> Northbrook, IL 60062
> Special education materials including audio cassettes, books, learning materials for daily living skills, physical education, recreation, science, health, and teacher training programs.

Humanics
>P.O. Box 7447
>Atlanta, GA 30309
>Materials and books focusing on parent involvement, early childhood
>and special education, and social services.

Human Sciences Press
>72 Fifth Avenue
>New York, NY 10011
>Books for parents, professionals, and children.

Ideal School Supply Co.
>11000 South Lavergne Avenue
>Oaklawn, IL 60453
>Materials for the development of sensory motor skills, language skills,
>and math skills; science activities for the visually handicapped; class-
>room equipment; preschool through elementary levels.

Imperial International Learning Corporation
>P.O. Box 548
>Kankakee, IL 60901
>Texts, materials and games for readiness and early childhood, reading,
>spelling and grammar, mathematics, science, social studies (K-8).

Inova
>Box 591
>State College, PA 16801
>Wooden toys.

Institute of Child-Centered Education
>Nova University
>3301 College Avenue
>Fort Lauderdale, FL 33314
>Resource books and educational toys for parents, preschool teachers,
>elementary teachers, and program directors/administrators.

Institute of Family Home Education
>P.O. Box 539
>Provo, UT 84057
>Brushing Up on Parenthood—Filmstrips and manual designed to help
>parents effectively teach children in the home.

Instructional/Communications Technology, Inc.
>10 Stepar Place
>Huntington Station
>New York, NY 11746
>Instructional devices, series, and materials for teaching reading, lis-
>tening, and learning skills from primary grades through adulthood, in-
>cluding special and bilingual education.

Instructional Objectives Exchange
        P.O. Box 24095
        Los Angeles, CA   90024
        Objectives-based test sets; measurable objectives collections, planning
        aids.

Interpretive Education
        2306 Winters Drive
        Kalamazoo, MI   49002
        Texts, filmstrips, programs in basic living skills; elementary-secondary.

JAB Press
        P.O. Box 39852
        Los Angeles, CA   90039
        Films, filmstrips, and cassette tape recordings for teacher training and
        parent orientation.

January Productions
        124 Rea Avenue
        Hawthorne, NJ   07506
        Pre-K-8 sound filmstrips and cassettes in health/safety, language arts,
        career/consumerism, social studies, science.

K & H Publishing Company
        3475 Via Oporto, Suite 204
        Newport Beach, CA   92663
        Special education survival skill/independent living texts.

Kaplan Corporation
        600 Jonestown Road
        P.O. Box 15027
        Winston-Salem, NC   27103
        Special education texts, materials, games in all subject areas for grades
        K-6.

Kids Come In Special Flavors, Co.
        Box 562 Forest Park Station
        Dayton, OH   45405
        Materials, texts, kits for special education.

Knowledge Tree Group
        360 Park Avenue South
        New York, NY   10010
        Media and materials for preschool through primary grades, in-service/
        teacher training, and parent education.

Kurtz Bros.
   Clearfield, PA 16830
   or
   Box L
   Paoli, PA 19301
   Instructo Learning Centers—language arts, metric, mathematics, social
   studies; "high interest, low level reading" large selection of special
   education materials.

Lakeshore Curriculum Materials Co.
   16463 Phoebe Avenue
   LaMirada, CA 90637
   Preschool through elementary level materials for active play, arts and
   crafts, role-play, tabletop play, perceptual skills, language arts,
   mathematics, science, and social studies; also books, furniture, posters,
   study prints, and teacher materials.

The Learning Business
   30961 Agoura Road
   Suite 325
   Westlake Village, CA 91361
   Language development materials; elementary level.

Learning Concepts
   2501 North Lamar
   Austin, TX 78705
   Programmed materials and kits, screening and diagnostic tests, cri-
   terion-referenced tests, mainstreaming materials for teachers, administrators, and parents.

The Learning Line
   Ladera Professional Center
   P.O. Box 1200
   Palo Alto, CA 94302
   Sullivan Educational Programs for reading readiness, reading, mathe-
   matics, science, and social science for kindergarten through secondary
   grades.

Learning Tree Filmstrips
   934 Pearl Street
   P.O. Box 1590, Department 100
   Boulder, CO 80302
   Filmstrips, cassettes, and teacher's guides for the areas of social
   studies, science, music, math, guidance, and career education; primary
   through junior high.

LEGO Systems, Inc.
    555 Taylor Road
    Enfield, CT 06082
    Building sets and accessories for nursery school through third grade.

Leswing Press
    750 Adrian Way
    San Rafael, CA 94903
    Educational materials including early learning kits, puppets, records,
    books, and games; grades K-5.

J. P. Lilley & Son, Inc.
    2009 North Third Street
    Box 3035
    Harrisburg, PA 17105
    16 mm commercial films.

LINC Services, Inc.
    Market Linkage Project for Special Education
    829 Eastwind Drive
    Westerville, OH 43081
    All types of materials, especially those produced in BEH funded projects,
    are made available.

J. B. Lippincott Co.
    Division of Higher Education
    East Washington Square
    Philadelphia, PA 19105
    Film series—Growth and Development: A Chronicle of Four Children;
    explores developmental question from a holistic viewpoint.

Lotto Talk, Inc.
    115 King Street
    Alexandria, VA 22314
    Language program materials for special education.

Love Publishing Co.
    6635 East Villanova Place
    Denver, CO 80222
    Materials include: books, spirit duplicating masters, resource room
    and learning center materials, special education teacher's kit, career
    education information, newsletters.

Lyons
    530 Riverview Avenue
    Elkhart, IN 46514
    Materials for all curriculum areas; preschool through primary grades
    and special education.

Macmillan Films, Inc.
: 34 MacQuesten Parkway South
Mount Vernon, NY 10550
16 mm films on art, dance, ecosystems and endangered species, health and safety, social documentaries, film study, fables, psychology, gardens and gardening, sports and recreation, children's films.

Macmillan Publishing Co., Inc.
: Front and Brown Streets
Riverside, NJ 08075
Materials in the areas of reading, English and language arts, early childhood, English as a second language, literature, music, and art.

Maddak, Inc.
: Pequannock, NJ 07440
Prosthetic aids for the handicapped, including daily living, home health care, rehabilitation, therapeutic, and laboratory equipment.

Markham Distributors, Inc.
: 507 Fifth Avenue
New York, NY 10017
Distributors of PLAYLEARN products for preschool through grade 3 and THERAPLAY products for use in special education programs.

McGraw-Hill Book Co.
: 1221 Avenue of the Americas
New York, NY 10020
Attn: Special Education Services/26th Floor
Wide selection of materials and services from McGraw-Hill for use in special education programs.

McGraw-Hill/Early Learning
: Paoli, PA 19301
Nontext materials and professional services focused on the areas of early childhood and primary education.

McGraw-Hill Films
: Department 443
1221 Avenue of the Americas
New York, NY 10020
"They Can Learn"—filmstrip series for teachers of children with learning disabilities.

Media Five
: 3211 Cahuenga Boulevard West
Hollywood, CA 90068
16 mm films and video cassettes for staff development and teacher training.

Media Materials, Inc.
>   Department K87654
>   2936 Remington Avenue
>   Baltimore, MD   21211
>   Cassette learning packages—all subjects; cassette activity books—
>   language arts, math, careers, and religious education; cassette learning
>   kits—language arts, math, read-a-longs.

Melton Book Co.
>   111 Leslie Street
>   Dallas, TX   75207
>   The RADEA Program—specific skills development program; comprehensive
>   curriculum for developmental ages 0-7. SAILS program for self-care and
>   independent living for secondary level students.

Charles E. Merrill Publishing Co.
>   College Division
>   1300 Alum Creek Drive/Box 508
>   Columbus, OH   43216
>   Special education textbooks.

Miller-Brody Productions
>   342 Madison Avenue
>   New York, NY   10017
>   Filmstrips, records, and cassettes for the areas of language arts,
>   social studies and cultural awareness, mathematics, science, and special
>   education; grades K-12.

Milton Bradley Co.
>   Springfield, MA   01101
>   GOAL: Early Learning Programs—Language development and mathematical
>   concepts for preschool and kindergarten levels.

Mind
>   181 Main Street
>   Norwalk, CT   06851
>   Survival Reading Program and Reading Technology Program for special
>   education.

Mind/Matter Corp.
>   P.O. Box 345
>   Danbury, CT   06810
>   Math, early childhood, language, and special education materials.

Modern Education Corporation
>   P.O. Box 721
>   Tulsa, OK   74101
>   Wide variety of resource materials for special education.

Modern Talking Picture Service
2323 New Hyde Park Road
New Hyde Park, NY 11040
16 mm free-loan films for adult groups.

The C.V. Mosby Company
11830 Westline Industrial Drive
St. Louis, MO 63141
Textbooks in special education.

Motor Development Equipment Co.
P.O. Box 4054
Downey, CA 90241
Motor development equipment for the mutliple-handicapped.

NASCO
901 Janesville Avenue
Fort Atkinson, WI 53538
Comprehensive line of teaching aids and supplies for preschool, special
education, and elementary levels.

National Association for the Education of Young Children
NAEYC
1834 Connecticut Avenue, N.W.
Washington, DC 20009
Publications for anyone involved in early childhood education.

National Audio Visual Center
Washington, DC 20409
Audiovisual programs for special education.

National Clearinghouse for Bilingual Education
1300 Wilson Boulevard
Suite B2-11
Rosslyn, VA 22209
Texts and information for teachers of bilingual students.

National Library Service for the Blind and Physically Handicapped
Library of Congress
Washington, DC 20542
Free reading program for blind and physically handicapped individuals,
including brailled and recorded books and magazines.

New Dimensions in Education, Inc.
16 DuPont Street
Plainview, NY 11803
Alpha One—a beginning readers program; grades K-3.

NOVO Educational Toy & Equipment Corp.
>124 West 24th Street
>New York, NY 10011
>Teaching aids, educational equipment, supplies, toys; preschool through grade 8.

Occupational Awareness
>Box 948
>Los Alamitos, CA 90720
>Special education career programs for secondary grades.

Open Court Publishing Company
>LaSalle, IL 61301
>Reading, language arts, and math series for regular and special education, bilingual, and gifted students.

PAR Project
>464 Central
>Northfield, IL 60093
>The Recipes for Fun series—activity books.

Parents' Magazine Films, Inc.
>52 Vanderbilt Avenue
>New York, NY 10017
>Sound-&-Color filmstrips in the areas of child development, parent education, family relationships, and children with special needs.

Pathscope Educational Media, Inc.
>71 Weyman Avenue
>New Rochelle, NY 10802
>Educational media and special education materials including math, career awareness, social studies, safety, early childhood, staff development, and texts.

Peacock Publishers
>401 West Irving Park Road
>Itasca, IL 60143
>Textbooks in education, psychology, sociology, social work.

A. W. Peller & Associates, Inc.
>Educational Materials
>124 Rea Avenue
>Hawthorne, NJ 07506
>Catalogs, texts, materials, duplicating books and masters, and games for grades K-6.

J. C. Penney Co., Inc.
> 1301 Avenue of the Americas
> New York, NY 10019
> Consumer education materials including magazines, filmstrips and other
> audiovisual materials, and consumer guides.

Perennial Education, Inc.
> 477 Roger Williams
> P.O. Box 855
> Ravinia
> Highland Park, IL 60035
> Wide variety of films, video cassettes, and filmstrips including parent-
> ing and special education for adults; also a series for elementary school
> children.

PlayLearn Products
> 2298 Grissom Drive
> St. Louis, MO 63141
> Indoor-outdoor materials for bilateral development, spatial judgment,
> hand-eye coordination, and general muscular development.

Portage Project Materials
> Cooperative Educational Service Agency 12
> 412 East Slifer Street
> Portage, WI 53901
> Portage curriculum for children, instructors, and parents.

Potomac Engineering Corp.
> 664 North Michigan Avenue
> Chicago, IL 60611
> Classroom furnishings, indoor activity equipment, art supplies, musical
> instruments, and outdoor activity equipment; preschool.

Prentice-Hall, Inc.
> Englewood Cliffs, NJ 07632
> College-level texts and professional books.

Prentke Romich Company
> R.D. 2, Box 191
> Shreve, OH 44676
> Electronic aids for the severely handicapped.

Prep Inc.
> 1575 Parkway Avenue
> Trenton, NJ 08628
> An audiovisual assessment of the major career education objectives;
> grades elementary through secondary.

Princeton Center for Infancy
    306 Alexander Street
    Princeton, NJ 08450
    Sleep/play equipment for infants and toddlers.

Promethean Films South
    P.O. Box 1489
    Auburn, AL 36830
    Teacher training films.

The Psychological Corp.
    757 Third Avenue
    New York, NY 10017
    Education tests and services, books, and professional publications;
    psychological tests and services, books, and professional publications.

Puppet Productions, Inc.
    P.O. Box 82008
    San Diego, CA 92138
    Hand puppets; accessories and program materials including cassettes,
    reel-to-reel tapes, videotapes, puppet stages, costumes, and scripts.

QED Productions
    P.O. Box 1608
    Burbank, CA 91505
    Economics for Primaries—filmstrip series with teacher's manual and
    poster.

Quercus Corporation
    2768 Pineridge Road
    Castro Valley, CA 94546
    Secondary special education soft texts in survival skills.

Random House School Division
    201 East 50th Street
    New York, NY 10022
    Basal and supplementary instructional materials at the elementary and
    secondary levels; texts; multimedia learning units; individualized
    skill building programs.

Reader's Digest Services, Inc.
    Educational Division
    Pleasantville, NY 10570
    Early Learning Modules/Piper Program:

Initial Experience	Visual Motor Processes
Perceptual Skills	Auditory Processes
Prereading	Language Skills
Number Concepts	Reasoning Abilities
Gross Motor Skills	

Reading Joy, Inc.
>P.O. Box 404
>Naperville, IL 60540
>Reading materials, games, and activities for kindergarten through grade 8.

Recreation Equipment Unlimited, Inc.
>P.O. Box 4700
>Pittsburgh, PA 15206
>Consultants, planners, distributors in physical education, playground, and athletic equipment.

Relevant Productions, Inc.
>1123 Seminole Street
>Clearwater, FL 33515
>Materials for secondary education stressing basic skills, career, consumer, adult basic education, remedial reading.

Research Press
>Box 317702
>Champaign, IL 61820
>Parenting programs—workshop materials, counseling programs, self-study manuals; some materials are also directed to teachers.

Rhythm Band, Inc.
>P.O. Box 126
>Fort Worth, TX 76101
>Rhythm instruments.

S & S Arts and Crafts
>Colchester, CT 06415
>Ideas and materials for therapy, education, and recreation.

St. Paul Book & Stationary Co.
>Box 3410
>St. Paul, MN 55165
>Complete line of school products for preschool through college.

Salco Toys Inc.
>Route 1
>Nerstrand, MN 55053
>Learning materials for toddlers and special needs children.

Scholastic
>904 Sylvan Avenue
>Englewood Cliffs, NJ 07632
>Early childhood materials including paperbacks, hardcover picture books, and audiovisual materials; preschool through third grade.

Scholastic's Higher Education Program
900 Sylvan Avenue
Englewood Cliffs, NJ 07632
Books, magazines, multimedia early childhood programs in bilingual
versions for Spanish-speaking students.

Science—A Process Approach
Xerox Education Sciences
555 Gotham Parkway
Carlstadt, NJ 07072
Science program for grades K through 6 that is designed to develop
skills in processes such as observing, measuring, and inferring.

Science Research Associates, Inc.
259 East Erie Street
Chicago, IL 60611
Educational materials for all curriculum areas, K-adult.

Scott, Foresman & Co.
1900 East Lake Avenue
Glenview, IL 60025
Materials include: reading systems, multisensory resource materials for
language arts, independent reading, survey tests, language program,
spelling program, handwriting/typing, dictionaries, English as a second
language, health, social studies, mathematics, foreign languages.

Selective Educational Equipment (See), Inc.
3 Bridge Street
Newton, MA 02195
Mathematics, science, and social science materials for grades K-12;
multimedia kit for elementary schools (grades 2-5) presents children with
a nonthreatening picture of what it might be like to have a disability;
teacher-training program for mainstreaming handicapped children into the
classroom includes filmstrip, cassette, teacher's guide.

SFA, James Stanfield Film Assoc.
Project: Adult
P.O. Box 851
Pasadena, CA 91102
Films and slide series—sex education curriculum for the mentally re-
tarded.

Silver Burdett Company
250 James Street
Morristown, NJ 07960
Texts and materials for language arts, mathematics, music, science,
social studies, school and public libraries; grades K-12.

Singer Education Division
    Career Systems
    80 Commerce Drive
    Rochester, NY 14623
    Programs for independent living, career systems.

Singer Society for Visual Education, Inc.
    1345 Diversey Parkway
    Chicago, IL 60614
    Filmstrips, records, cassettes, and slides for language arts, science,
    mathematics, career education, and social studies; holiday program
    materials; primary through junior high.

Skill Development Equipment Co.
    Box 6300
    1340 North Jefferson
    Anaheim, CA 92807
    Exercise and relaxation equipment for infants, children, and adults;
    appropriate for special education programs.

Society for Visual Education, Inc.
    SVE Multimedia Catalog, Pre-Primary
    1345 Diversey Parkway
    Chicago, IL 60614
    Preprimary, elementary upper grades.

Special Education Associates
    P.O. Box 9497
    Austin, TX 78766
    Child Study Team Training Program—focuses on effective group strate-
    gies for the implementation of P.L. 94-142 and individualized education
    programs.

STEP
    School Teacher's Educational Products, Inc.
    South Complex Paine Field
    Everett, WA 98204
    Reading readiness, math development, and learning motivation materials
    for early childhood, elementary levels, and special education.

Sterling Educational Films
    241 East 34th Street
    New York, NY 10016
    Child development film series.

TADS

>500 NC NB Plaza
>Chapel Hill, NC 27514
>Publishes Cycles, a bimonthly publication of the First Chance Network;
>First Chance projects are designed to develop and demonstrate effective
>approaches in assisting preschool children with handicaps.

Teachers College Press

>1234 Amsterdam Avenue
>New York, NY 10027
>Books; cognitive skills assessment battery.

Teachers Publishing

>100 F. Brown Street
>Riverside, NJ 08075
>Activity books and other teaching aids for all subjects; preschool
>through grade 12.

Teaching Pathways

>P.O. Box 31582
>Amarillo, TX 79120
>Nongraded and noncategorical curriculum guides for handicapped students
>at the secondary level, and a teacher training course.

Teaching Resources Corporation

>100 Boylston Street
>Boston, MA 02116
>Materials for special learning situations including tests, language de-
>velopment, basic programs, basic materials, mathematics, in-service
>filmstrips.

Telesensory Systems, Inc.

>3408 Hillview Avenue
>P.O. Box 10099
>Palo Alto, CA 94304
>Electrical and electronic equipment for handicapped individuals: Optacon,
>converting the image of a printed letter into a tactile form for blind
>people; Autocom, a portable electronic language board for deaf and physi-
>cally handicapped people; Crib-O-Gram, being used to detect hearing im-
>pairment among newborn babies; electric braille; and others.

Toy Review

>P.O. Box 176
>Newton, MA 02160
>Information and opinion magazine about children's toys.

TREND Enterprises
>   Box 3073
>   St. Paul, MN 55165
>   Bulletin board sets, posters, educational games, and early childhood
>   readiness kits; preschool through elementary levels.

Troubador Press
>   385 Fremont Street
>   San Francisco, CA 94105
>   Creative enrichment centers for the gifted and talented.

United Canvas & Sling, Inc.
>   248 River Street
>   Hackensack, NJ 07601
>   Equipment for the development of perceptual-motor skills.

University Park Press
>   233 East Redwood Street
>   Baltimore, MD 21202
>   Textbooks for special education.

VMI Media for Learning
>   Menlo Park, CA 94025
>   Teacher duplicator books, transparency/duplicator books, grade level
>   sets, "super" duplicator books, "drillmaster" learning arithmetic
>   modules—in areas of reading, language arts, social studies books,
>   science, math; K-secondary.

Vort Corporation
>   P.O. Box 11552
>   Palo Alto, CA 94306
>   Practical tools for implementing P.L. 94-142 and Section 504.

V.R. Data Corporation
>   777 Henderson Boulevard, N-6
>   Folcroft, PA 19032
>   Comprehensive IEP report management system.

Walker Educational Book Corp.
>   720 Fifth Avenue
>   New York, NY 10019
>   Perceptual Skills Curriculum—an individualized program for teaching
>   children the basic perceptual abilities necessary for elementary level
>   reading, arithmetic, handwriting, and spelling programs.

Walt Disney Educational Media Co.
>   500 South Buena Vista Street
>   Burbank, CA 91521
>   Filmstrips, study prints, records, and multimedia programs for all
>   curriculum areas; grades K-8.

Webster International, Inc.
> 5724 Cloverland Place
> Brentwood (Nashville), TN 27027
> Materials for parent training and involvement.

Webster/McGraw-Hill
> 30th Floor
> 1221 Avenue of the Americas
> New York, NY 10020
> Instructional materials for all curriculum areas; grades K-12;
> professional and reference books.

Western Psychological Services
> 12031 Wilshire Boulevard
> Los Angeles, CA 90025
> Standardized tests, selected books, personnel forms, apparatus, and
> timing devices for the professions of psychology, education, special
> education, medicine, personnel, rehabilitation, and research.

Weston Woods
> Weston, CT 06883
> Books, filmstrips, and cassettes for preschool through intermediate
> grades.

Wiley Professional Books-By-Mail
> John Wiley & Sons, Inc.
> P.O. Box 063
> Somerset, NJ 08873
> Psychology books—professional and textbooks.

Winston Press
> 430 Oak Grove
> Minneapolis, MN 55403
> Human development materials in values and moral growth for children and
> adults.

Wombat Productions, Inc.
> 77 Tarrytown Road
> White Plains, NY 10607
> Films appropriate for use in the fields of humanities, social studies,
> language arts, guidance, and filmic art.

Xerox Education Publications
> 1250 Fairwood Avenue
> P.O. Box 16629
> Columbus, OH 43216
> Texts and materials in all subject areas including career education,
> bilingual education, and filmstrips (K-12).

Organizations

Alexander Graham Bell Association
  for the Deaf
3417 Volta Place, N.W.
Washington, DC 20007

American Academy for Cerebral Palsy
1255 New Hampshire Avenue, N.W.
Washington, DC 20036

American Association of Elementary-
  Kindergarten-Nursery Educators
1202 16th Street, N.W.
Washington, DC 20036

American Association for Gifted
  Children
15 Gramercy Park
New York, NY 10003

American Association for Health,
  Physical Education, and Recreation
1201 16th Street, N.W.
Washington, DC 20036

American Association on Mental
  Deficiency
5101 Wisconsin Avenue, N.W.
Washington, DC 20016

American Association of Psychiatric
  Clinics for Children
250 West 57th Street
New York, NY 10019

American Association of Psychiatric
  Services for Children
1701 18th Street, N.W.
Washington, DC 20009

American Association of School
  Administrators
1801 North Moore Street
Arlington, VA 22209

American Association of Workers for
  The Blind
1511 K Street, N.W.
Washington, DC 20005

American Coalition of Citizens with
  Disabilities
1346 Connecticut Avenue, N.W., #817
Washington, DC 20036

American Council for the Blind
1211 Connecticut Avenue, N.W.
Washington, DC 20006

American Educational Research Association
1126 16th Street, N.W.
Washington, DC 20006

American Foundation for the Blind
16 West 16th Street
New York, NY 10011

American Humane Association
Children's Division
P.O. Box 1266
Denver, CO 80201

American Library Association
110 Maryland Avenue, N.E., Box 54
Washington, DC 20002

American Occupational Therapy Association
6000 Executive Boulevard, Suite 200
Rockville, MD 20852

American Orthopsychiatric Association
1775 Broadway
New York, NY   10019

American Personnel and Guidance
  Association
1607 New Hampshire Avenue, N.W.
Washington, DC   20009

American Physical Therapy Association
1156 15th Street, N.W., Suite 500
Washington, DC   20005

American School Health Association
Kent, OH   44240

American Society for Public
  Administration
1225 Connecticut Avenue, N.W.
Washington, DC   20036

American Speech, Language and
  Hearing Association
10801 Rockville Pike
Rockville, MD   20852

American Vocational Association
2020 North 14th Street
Arlington, VA   22201

Architectural Barriers Committee
National Association of the
  Physically Handicapped
6473 Grandville
Detroit, MI   48228

Association for Childhood Education
  International
3615 Wisconsin Avenue, N.W.
Washington, DC   20016

Association for Children with
  Learning Disabilities
4156 Library Road
Pittsburgh, PA   15234

Association for Education of the
  Visually Handicapped
919 Walnut Street
San Francisco, CA   94121

The Association for the Severely
  Handicapped
1600 West Armory Way
Seattle, WA   98119

Association for Supervision and
  Curriculum Development
1701 K Street, N.W.
Washington, DC   20006

Black Child Development Institute
1028 Connecticut Avenue, N.W.
Suite 514
Washington, DC   20036

Center for Independent Living, Inc.
2539 Telegraph Avenue
Berkeley, CA   94704

Center for Innovation in Teaching
  the Handicapped
Indiana University
2805 East 10th Street
Bloomington, IN   47401

Child Study Association of America
9 East 89th Street
New York, NY   10028

Child Welfare League of America
67 Irving Place
New York, NY   10003

Children's Defense Fund
1520 New Hampshire Avenue, N.W.
Washington, DC   20036

Children's Foundation
1026 Seventeenth Street, N.W.
Washington, DC   20036

Closer Look—National Information
  Center for Handicapped
Box 1492
Washington, DC   20013

Conference of Executives of American
  Schools for the Deaf
5034 Wisconsin Avenue, N.W.
Washington, DC   20016

Convention of American Instructors
  of the Deaf, Inc.
5034 Wisconsin Avenue, N.W., Suite 11
Washington, DC   20016

Co-Ordinating Council for Handicapped Children
407 South Dearborn, Room 400
Chicago, IL   60605

Council of Administrators of
  Special Education
1920 Association Drive
Reston, VA   22091

Council for Educational Development
  and Research
1518 K Street, N.W., #206
Washington, DC   20005

Council for Exceptional Children
1920 Association Drive
Reston, VA   22091

Council of State Administrators of
  Vocational Rehabilitation
1522 K Street, N.W., #610
Washington, DC   20005

Creative Education Foundation
State University College at Buffalo
218 Chase Hall,
1300 Elmwood Avenue
Buffalo, NY   14222

Cystic Fibrosis Foundation
3379 Peachtree Road, N.E., Suite 950
Atlanta, GA   30326

Day Care and Child Development
  Council of America
1401 K Street, N.W.
Washington, DC   20005

Dental Guidance Council for Cerebral
  Palsy
122 East 23rd Street
New York, NY   10010

Education Commission of the States
444 North Capitol Street, N.W.
Suite 321
Washington, DC   20001

Educational Development Center
55 Chapel Street
Cambridge, MA   02138

Educational Facilities Laboratories
477 Madison Avenue
New York, NY   10022

Epilepsy Foundation of America
1828 L Street, N.W.
Washington, DC   20036

Family Services Association of
  America
44 East 23rd Street
New York, NY   10010

International League of Societies for
  the Mentally Retarded
12 Rue Forestiere
Brussels 5, Belgium

International Reading Association
800 Barksdale Road, P.O.B. 8139
Newark, DE   19711

Joint Commission on Mental Health
  of Children
5454 Wisconsin Avenue
Chevy Chase, MD   20015

League Against Child Abuse
21 East State Street
Columbus, OH 43215

Library of Congress National Library
  Services for the Visually and
  Physically Handicapped
1291 Taylor Street, N.W.
Washington, DC 20542

Mental Health Materials Center—
  Human Relations Aide
419 Park Avenue South
New York, NY 10016

Merrill-Palmer Institute
51 East Ferry Avenue
Detroit, MI 48202

Muscular Dystrophy Associations
810 Seventh Avenue
New York, NY 10019

National Association of Administrators of State & Federal
  Education Programs
1902 Lundwood Avenue
Ann Arbor, MI 40103

National Association of the Deaf
814 Thayer Avenue
Silver Spring, MD 20910

National Association of the Deaf-
  Blind
2703 Forest Oak Circle
Norman, OK 73071

National Association for the
  Education of Young Children
1834 Connecticut Avenue, N.W.
Washington, DC 20009

National Association of Elementary
  School Principals
1801 North Moore Street
Arlington, VA 22209

National Association of ESEA Title I
  Coordinators
Iowa Office of Public Instruction
Grimes Office Building
Des Moines, IO 50319

National Association of Hearing and
  Speech Action
814 Thayer Avenue
Silver Spring, MD 20910

National Association for Mental
  Health
10 Columbus Circle
New York, NY 10019

National Association of the Physically Handicapped
76 Elm Street
London, OH 43140

National Association of Private
  Residential Facilities for the
  Mentally Retarded
6269 Leesburg Pike
Falls Church, VA 22044

National Association of Private
  Schools for Exceptional Children
7700 Miller Road
Miami, FL 33155

National Association for Retarded
  Citizens
2709 Avenue E East
P.O. Box 6109
Arlington, TX 76011

National Association of School
  Psychologists
1246 Maryland Avenue, N.E.
Washington, DC 20002

National Association of Secondary
  School Principals
1904 Association Drive
Reston, VA 22091

National Association of State Boards
of Education
444 North Capital Street, N.W.
Suite 526
Washington, DC   20001

National Association of State
Directors of Special Education
1510 H Street, N.W., Suite 301C
Washington, DC   20005

National Association for the
Visually Handicapped
3201 Balboa Street
San Francisco, CA   94121

National Audio Visual Association
3150 Spring Street
Fairfax, VA   22031

National Center for the Prevention
and Treatment of Child Abuse
and Neglect
1205 Oneida Street
Denver, CO   80220

National Committee for Citizens in
Education
2415 Davis Avenue
Alexandria, VA   22303

National Congress of Parents and
Teachers
1201 16th Street, N.W.
Washington, DC   20036

National Education Association
1201 16th Street, N.W.
Washington, DC   20036

National Epilepsy League, Inc.
6 North Michigan Avenue
Chicago, IL   60602

National Federation for the Blind
Suite 212, Dupont Circle Building
1346 Connecticut Avenue, N.W.
Washington, DC   20036

National Foundation, The March of
Dimes
School Relations & Health Education
Box 2000
White Plains, NY   10602

National Headquarters for Mental
Health Association
1800 North Kent Street
Rosslyn, VA   22209

National Institute of Child Health
and Human Development
National Institute of Health
Building 31, Room 2A34
Bethesda, MD   20014

National Institute of Mental Health
5454 Wisconsin Avenue
Chevy Chase, MD   20015

National Center on Education Media
and Materials for the Handicapped
Ohio State University
Columbus, OH   43210

National Kindergarten Association
8 West 40th Street
New York, NY   10018

National Paraplegia Foundation
333 North Michigan Avenue
Chicago, IL   60601

National Quadriplegia Foundation
333 North Michigan Avenue
Chicago, IL   60601

National Rehabilitation Association
1522 K Street, N.W., Suite 1120
Washington, DC   20005

National School Supply & Equipment
Association
1500 Wilson Boulevard, Suite 609
Arlington, VA   22209

National Society for Autistic
  Children
169 Tampa Avenue
Albany, NY 12208

National Society for Crippled
  Children and Adults (Easter
  Seal Society)
2023 West Ogden Avenue
Chicago, IL 60612

National Society to Prevent
  Blindness, Inc.
79 Madison Avenue
New York, NY 10016

National Therapeutic Recreation
  Society
c/o National Recreation and Park
  Association
1601 North Kent Street
Arlington, VA 22209

National Urban League
425 13th Street, N.W.
Washington, DC 20004

The President's Committee on Mental
  Retardation
Department of Health, Education,
  and Welfare
Room 2614
Washington, DC 20201

Research for Better Schools
1700 Market Street
Philadelphia, PA 19103

Society for Research in Child
  Development
University of Chicago
5801 Ellis Avenue
Chicago, IL 60637

Society for Visual Education
1345 Diversey Parkway
Chicago, IL 60614

Spina Bifida Association of America
343 South Dearborn Street, Room 319
Chicago, IL 60604

State Higher Education Executive
  Officers
One American Place, Suite 1530
Baton Rouge, LA 70825

United Cerebral Palsy Association
66 East 34th Street
New York, NY 10016

Vision Conservation Institute, Inc.
P.O. Box 2591
Sacramento, CA 95812

Films

Abbey's First Two Years. B/W, 30 minutes
    Modern Talking Picture Service
    1212 Avenue of the Americas, New York, NY 10036
    Study of human development, with very specific insights into language,
    and the growth of emotional and intellectual concepts.

The Adolescent Iliad. 1970, color, 25 minutes
    Lawren Publications, Inc.
    P.O. Box 1542, Burlingame, CA 94010
    Demonstrates new methods of treating emotionally disturbed teenagers.

All My Buttons. 1973, color, 28 minutes
    H & H Enterprises, Inc.
    P.O. Box 1070, Lawrence, KS 66044
    Illustrates contemporary problems associated with the normalization of
    developmentally disabled citizens.

. . . And So They Learn. 1972, color, 35 minutes
    Pennsylvania Department of Education
    Box 911, Harrisburg, PA 17126
    Four approaches to early childhood education: a modified Bereiter-
    Engleman approach, a team-teaching kindergarten, a Montessori school,
    and a one-teacher public school classroom.

Anybody's Child: Parts 1 and 2. 1975, color, 49 minutes
    The Moving Picture Company
    P.O. Box 263, Oregon City, OR 97045
    Overview of reading and writing problems of the school-age child;
    development of remedial techniques.

Applied Behavior Analysis Research Designs. 1974, color, 40 minutes
    H & H Enterprises, Inc.
    P.O. Box 1070, Lawrence KS 66044
    Three behavioral researchers talk about why it was necessary to develop
    applied behavior analysis; what makes it work, results, and some impli-
    cations of the method in changing the social system.

Approaches to Early Childhood Curriculum. 1968, 25 minutes
    Anti-Defamation League of B'nai B'rith
    315 Lexington Avenue, New York, NY   10016
    Three short sequences at the preschool level are used to explain the
    Institute for Developmental Study's method for teaching abstract con-
    cepts, self-image development, and how games can reinforce learning.

Art with Multiple-Handicapped Blind Children. "We'll Show You What We're
Gonna Do!" 1974, B/W with color sequences, 27 minutes
    ACI Media, Inc.
    35 West 45th Street, New York, NY   10036
    Exploratory art program for blind, partially sighted, and other handi-
    capped children at the Western Pennsylvania School for Blind Children.

Ask Just for Little Things. 1972, color, 20 minutes
    Hallmark Films & Recordings
    1511 East North Avenue, Baltimore, MD   21213
    Parent is shown how to train child in a home setting, using program
    based on fundamental concepts of behavior modification.

Audiological Procedures with Preschool Deaf Children. 1967, 30 minutes
    The Pennsylvania State University, Department of Audiovisual Services
    Special Services Building, University Park, PA   16802
    Emphasizes audiological procedures, leading to different diagnosis, and
    the use of extensive descriptions of each child's auditory status.

Autism's Lonely Children. 1965, 20 minutes
    Indiana University, Audiovisual Center
    Bloomington, IN   47401
    Shows attempts to teach children to talk and identify objects for the
    first time.

Behavior Modification in the Classroom. 1970, color, 24 minutes
    University of California, Extension Media Center
    Berkeley, CA   94720
    Use of operant conditioning and modeling procedures to help children
    become more task-oriented.

Behavior Modification: Teaching Language to Psychotic Children. 1969, color,
42 minutes
    Prentice-Hall, Inc., Film Library
    Englewood Cliffs, NJ   07632
    Ivan Lovaas shows reinforcement and stimulus fading techniques in
    teaching speech to psychotic children.

Being. 1973, color, 21 minutes
    ACI Media, Inc.
    35 West 45th Street, New York, NY 10035
    A young man, paralyzed in both legs, confuses friendship for pity.

Blindness Is. 1966, 27 minutes
    University of Iowa, Audio Visual Center
    C-5 East Hall, Iowa City, IA 52240
    Blindness explained from the point of view of the blind.

Born to Succeed: Part 1—The Concept of Number. 1971, color, 32 minutes
    Prentice-Hall, Inc., Film Library
    Englewood Cliffs, NJ 07632
    Demonstrates the application of teaching theories developed by behavioral
    psychologists to specific techniques of accelerating learning in re-
    tarded children.

Born to Succeed: Part 2—Arithmetic. 1971, color, 30 minutes
    Prentice-Hall, Inc., Film Library
    Englewood Cliffs, NJ 07632
    Shows how children with a mental age of 5½ can be trained to do
    arithmetic.

Boy Named Terry Egan. 1973, color, 52 minutes
    Carousel Films, Inc.
    1501 Broadway, New York, NY 10036
    Explores problems, symptoms, and possibilities for treatment of autistic
    children.

The Brain-Damaged Child. 1967, 31 minutes
    The Pennsylvania State University, Department of Audiovisual Services
    Special Services Building, University Park, PA 16802
    Interview between psychiatrist and 7-year-old Bobby, a boy with organic
    brain damage.

Branded Imperfect. 1976, color, 14 minutes
    National Audio Visual Center, General Services Administration
    Washington, DC 20409
    This film follows the progress, diagnosis, and adaptation to the condi-
    tion of a young construction worker who suffers his first epileptic
    seizure on the job.

Broken Bones, Broken Homes. 1974, Part I—30 minutes, Part II—60 minutes,
color
    Communications Specialists, National Center for Juvenile Justice
    1309 Cathedral of Learning, Pittsburgh, PA 15260
    Reviews historical, psychiatric, legal, public welfare and research
    aspects of problems of abuse and neglect.

The Broken Bridge. 1969, color, 35 minutes
     Time-Life Films, Inc., 16 MM. Department
     43 West 16th Street, New York, NY 10011
     Teaches parents how to apply operant conditioning to their severely
     troubled children.

Can I Come Back Tomorrow? 1973, color, 33 minutes
     California State University, LB P P
     5151 State College Drive, Los Angeles, CA 90032
     Shows how competent teachers with contrasting styles teach children with
     learning disabilities in a self-contained classroom.

Cast No Shadow. 1973, color, 27 minutes
     Professional Arts, Inc.
     Box 8003, Stanford, CA 94305
     Recreation activities for severely mentally retarded, physically handi-
     capped, multihandicapped, and emotionally disturbed children, teens,
     adults.

Child Behavior = You. 1973, color, 15 minutes
     Benchmark Films, Inc.
     145 Scarborough Road, Briarcliff Manor, NY 10510
     Humorous animation shows parent-child relations and methods of modifying
     behavior.

Child of the Future: Parts I and II. 1966, 57 minutes
     Contemporary/McGraw-Hill Films, Sales Service Department
     1221 Avenue of the Americas, New York, NY 10020
     Teaching techniques that give children personal involvement in the sub-
     jects they are learning, allow children to be individuals, and speed up
     the learning process.

A Child Is A Child. 1973, color, 7 minutes
     Aims Instructional Media Service
     P.O. Box 1010, Hollywood, CA 90028
     Shows children with handicaps integrated with nonhandicapped children in
     a preschool laboratory.

Child of the Universe. 1973, color, 30 minutes
     Robin Miller, Filmmaker
     Bethlehem, PA 18018
     The fears and suspicions of the retarded. A commentary by parents of the
     mentally retarded and retarded adults in society.

Children at Risk. 1968, color, 30 minutes
    Franklin Institute Research Lab
    20th and Race Streets, Philadelphia, PA 19103
    Intervention program for preschoolers; shows professionals from different
    disciplines working with the child, the referring teacher, and the
    parents.

Count Me In. 1976, color, 16 mm 20 minutes
    Stanfield House Films
    P.O. Box 3208, Santa Monica, CA 90403
    Shows developmentally disabled person involved in independent living,
    work, and recreation, and explains how the handicapped can achieve a
    productive and fulfilling life.

The Curb Between Us. 1975, color, 15 minutes
    Arthur Barr Productions, P.O. Box 7-C
    1029 North Allen Avenue, Pasadena, CA 91104
    A disabled adolescent as he rebuilds his life after an accident.

Daddy, Can I Hear the Sun? 1978, color, 27 minutes
    Stanfield House Films/Media
    12381 Wilshire Boulevard, Suite 203, Los Angeles, CA 90025
    The meaning and advantage of total communication for the deaf.

Danny and Nicky. 1969, color, 55 minutes
    Films Incorporated
    1144 Wilmette Avenue, Wilmette, IL 60091
    Compares institutional and home care of mentally retarded children.

A Day in the Life of Bonnie Consolo. 1975, color, 16½ minutes
    Arthur Barr Productions, P.O. Box 7-C
    1029 North Allen Avenue, Pasadena, CA 91104
    How a woman without arms manages her life, showing her ingenious
    self-sufficiency.

Development of the Child: Cognition. 1972, color, 30 minutes
    Harper & Row, Publishers
    10 East 53rd Street, New York, NY 10022
    Addresses problem solving in terms of perception, memory, evaluation,
    and reasoning.

Development of the Child: Language Development. 1972, color, 20 minutes
    Harper & Row, Publishers
    10 East 53rd Street, New York, NY 10022
    Topics included are: child's language processes in the first four years,
    process by which language is acquired, and how acquisition can be in-
    fluenced.

Discipline and Self-Control. B/W, 20 minutes
    Modern Talking Picture Service
    1212 Avenue of the Americas, New York, NY 10036
    Discusses the problem of discipline in teaching and living with young
    children. Spanish translation available.

Early Recognition of Learning Disabilities. 1969, color, 30 minutes
    Audio Visual Center
    6422 West Lake Street, Minneapolis, MN 55426
    Emphasizes the urgent need to recognize and accept learning disabilities
    early, provide extra teaching needed to overcome these disabilities, and
    get communities to provide facilities for extra help.

Ears to Hear. 1975, color, 28 minutes
    Filmmakers Library, Inc.
    133 East 58th Street, Suite 703A, New York, NY 10022
    Auditory method of therapy shows how profoundly deaf children can be
    taught to speak normally and to "hear" the sounds of ordinary speech.

Educated Hands. 1965, color, 11 minutes
    West Virginia University, Audio-Visual Library
    Department of Radio, Television, Motion Pictures, Morgantown, WV 26506
    Value of industrial arts training to mentally retarded children.

Epileptic Seizure Patterns. 1963, color, 25 minutes
    Indiana University, Audiovisual Center
    Bloomington, IN 47401
    Historical aspects of epilepsy; various types of seizures.

Evaluation by the School Psychologist. 1977, color, 20 minutes
    Instructional Media Services
    128 East Pittsburgh Street, Greensburg, PA 15601
    Traces evaluation procedure from a teacher's referral of a student who
    is having difficulty in school to acquisition of the special education
    help needed by the pupil.

The Exceptional Child. 1967, 51 minutes
    Time-Life Multimedia Division
    100 Eisenhower Drive, Paramus, NJ 07652
    Exceptional children include the gifted, those suffering neurological
    difficulties, the dyslectic, and the stutterer. What causes these con-
    ditions and how disabilities should be treated.

Exceptional Times: An Historical Perspective of Special Education. 1977,
color, 14 minutes
    Council for Exceptional Children
    1920 Association Drive, Reston, VA 22091
    Overview of some of the significant events in the history of special
    education.

First Steps. 1976, color, 24 minutes
  Contemporary/McGraw-Hill Films, Sales Service Department
  110 15th Street, Del Mar, CA 92014
  Documents three growing trends in teaching the educably mentally retarded: retention in the home, early childhood skill development training, and mainstreaming of school-age children into regular classrooms.

The First Ten Months of Life: Part I. 27 minutes.
  McGraw-Hill Book Company
  Princeton Road, Hightstown, NJ 08520
  Common problems of premature infants are analyzed.

Fitting In. 1977, color, 27 minutes
  University of Wisconsin, Extension Bureau of AV Instruction
  1327 University Avenue, P.O. Box 2093, Madison, WI 53708
  Myths about epilepsy, cerebral palsy, and mental retardation are
  examined. Portrays three disabled persons who are leading productive
  lives in their communities.

Fulfillment of Human Potential. 1980, color, 18 minutes
  McGraw-Hill
  1221 Avenue of the Americas, New York, NY 10020
  Illustrates the process of teacher sensitization to the handicapped
  child. Shows children mainstreamed into laboratory science class and
  related art activities.

Genesis. 1971, color, 25 minutes
  Hallmark Films
  1511 East North Avenue, Baltimore, MD 21213
  How to train children in basic self-help skills: dressing, eating, and
  toileting.

Graduation. 1973, color, 17 minutes
  Stanfield House
  900 Euclid Avenue, P.O. Box 3208, Santa Monica, CA 90403
  Personal interviews with parents and guardians explore the question,
  "What happens to the retarded child when he grows up?"

Growing Up With Deafness. 1962, color, 31 minutes
  Classroom Films Distributors, Inc.
  5610 Hollywood Boulevard, Los Angeles, CA 90028
  Demonstrates that those who have been born deaf can become confident,
  well-adjusted people with the ability to communicate.

Growth and Development of a Multiple-Handicapped Infant. 1969, 10 minutes
  New York University, Audio Visual Center
  26 Washington Place, New York, NY 10003
  Documents first $3\frac{1}{2}$ years of a profoundly retarded blind infant.

Hearing Assessment for the Young and Difficult to Test. 1975, color,
12 minutes
　　　University of Kansas Audiovisual Center
　　　Lawrence, Kansas 66044
　　　Demonstrates the use of operant audiometric techniques.

He Comes From Another Room. 1974, color, 27 minutes
　　　National Audiovisual Center
　　　General Services Administration, Washington, D.C. 20409
　　　Excerpts of a program for integrating emotionally disturbed children
　　　into the mainstream of a regular third-grade classroom.

Helpers: Personalizing the Teaching of Reading.
　　　Agency for Instructional Television
　　　Box a, Bloomington, IN 47402
　　　Paid aides, community volunteers, and student tutors provide individual
　　　reading instruction when they are trained and teachers are prepared to
　　　work with them.

Help for Mark. 1970, color, 17 minutes
　　　Appleton-Century-Croft
　　　440 Park Avenue South, New York, NY 10016
　　　Introduces principles of behavior modification for parents and teachers.

Hidden Handicaps. Color, 23 minutes
　　　McGraw-Hill
　　　1221 Avenue of the Americas, New York, NY 10020
　　　Introduction to learning disabilities, diagnosis, and treatment
　　　approaches.

The How and What of Sex Education for Educables. 1975, color, 20 minutes
　　　Hallmark Films
　　　1511 East North Avenue, Baltimore, MD 21213
　　　Shows actual scenes of situations and how they should be handled.

The Hyperactive Child. 1969, color, 34 minutes
　　　CIBA Pharmaceutical Co., Medical Communications Department
　　　556 Morris Avenue, Summit, NJ 07901
　　　Explains the causes of hyperactivity and professional management by
　　　medical and scholastic communities.

The Iceberg Stuttering. 1968, 60 minutes
　　　University of California, LA, UCLA Instructional Media Library
　　　405 Hilgard Avenue, Royce Hall #8, Los Angeles, CA 90024
　　　The nature of stuttering; experimental therapy; practical therapeutic
　　　approaches using monitoring, role taking, group psychotherapy, and
　　　behavior modification.

Identifying Speech Disorders: Articulation Disorders. 1972, 20 minutes
     Harper & Row, Publisher
     10 East 53rd Street, New York, NY 10022
     Series of interviews with subjects displaying deviant behavior in
     language comprehension and oral language production.

Identifying Speech Disorders: Stuttering. 1972, 20 minutes
     Harper & Row, Publisher
     10 East 53rd Street, New York, NY 10022
     Series of interviews with subjects displaying disruptions in speech
     such as repetition, unnatural silences, prolongation of sounds, intense
     struggling to speak, all of which are characteristic of stuttering.

Identifying Speech Disorders: Voice and Resonance Disorders. 1972, 20 minutes
     Harper & Row, Publisher
     10 East 53rd Street, New York, NY 10022
     Information about various disorders including severe breathiness, cleft
     palate, esophageal voice production, hypernasality, papillomas and
     postlaryngectomy therapy.

I.E.P.: The Individualized Education Program. 1977, color, 22 minutes
     Instructional Media Services
     128 East Pittsburgh Street, Greensburg, PA 15601
     An introduction to the development, implementation, and review of an
     IEP, the right to due process proceedings, placement, and the program
     planning conference.

I'll Find a Way. 1977, color, 26 minutes
     The Media Guild
     Box 881, Solano Beach, CA 92075
     Provides insight into how a 9-year-old girl born with spina bifida
     functions and how she likes to be treated.

I'll Promise You A Tomorrow. 1972, color, 20 minutes
     Hallmark Films & Recordings, Inc.
     1511 East North Avenue, Baltimore, MD 21213
     Demonstrates the basic concepts of orienting an exceptional child to
     the community and shows the viewer how to teach some necessary life
     skills.

Impact of a Teacher's Behavior on Learners and Learning—John Withall. 1969,
71 minutes
     The Pennsylvania State University, Department of Audiovisual Services
     Special Services Building, University Park, PA 16802
     Two instructional modes emphasize the impact of the teacher's verbal
     and nonverbal behavior on learners, with guidelines for systematic
     analysis of teaching behavior.

Infant Appraisal. 1973, color, 27 minutes
    National Audio Visual Center
    General Services Administration, Washington, DC 20409
    This film emphasizes the need for early identification of handicapping
    conditions in infants.

In the Mainstream. 1979, color, 14 minutes
    Carousel Films, Inc.
    1501 Broadway, New York, NY 10036
    Examines how P.L. 94-142, which mandates that all handicapped children be
    educated at public expense and in the same classroom with other children
    whenever possible, is working.

Intelligence: A Complex Concept. 1980, color, 20 minutes
    CRM, McGraw-Hill Films
    110 Fifteenth Street, Del Mar, CA 92014
    Discusses definitions of intelligence, problems inherent in testing,
    and types of tests available.

It's Cool To Be Smart. 1980, color, 23 minutes
    McGraw-Hill
    1221 Avenue of the Americas, New York, NY 10020
    Shows programs for the gifted and suggests that the U.S. should put more
    effort into this area.

It's Their World, Too. 1976, color, 22 minutes
    National Audio Visual Center
    General Services Administration, Washington, DC 20409
    Overviews some of the lifestyles of retarded citizens by showing three
    actual situations.

The Invisible Handicap. 1976, color, 15 minutes
    Carousel Films, Inc.
    1501 Broadway, New York, NY 10036
    A "60 Minute" program on problems of learning disabilities.

James & John. Color, 23 minutes
    Peach Enterprises, Inc.
    4649 Gerald, Warren, MI 48092
    How a resourceful family provided for the needs of mongoloid twins in
    the home.

Jamie: A Behavioral Approach to Family Intervention. 1976, color, 17 minutes
    The Media Guild
    Box 881, Solano Beach, CA 92075
    Case study of a behavior modification program used to control childhood
    aggression.

Janet Is A Little Girl. 1972, B/W, 28 minutes
    University of California, Extension Media Center
    2223 Fulton Street, Berkeley, CA 94720
    Observes severely retarded Down's Syndrome children who were part of an
    innovative program at a California state mental hospital.

Job Interview: I Guess, I Got the Job. 1975, color, 13 minutes
    McGraw-Hill Films
    1221 Avenue of the Americas, New York, NY 10020
    Shows two boys taking very different approaches to a job interview.
    Examines whether honesty or personal salesmanship is the best tack, and
    explains nonverbal language in interviews.

Joey. 1974, B/W, 70 minutes
    Time-Life Films, Inc., 16 MM. Department
    43 West 16th Street, New York, NY 10011
    Story of Joey Deacon, a severely disabled spastic man, unable to walk
    or talk.

Just For the Fun Of It. 1970, color, 20 minutes
    Aims Instructional Media Services, Inc.
    P.O. Box 1010, Hollywood, CA 90028
    Series of physical activities for mentally handicapped children,
    ranging from simple to complex.

Kirsten Learns to Eat. 1971, color, 10 minutes
    Oregon State System of Higher Education, Audio-Visual Services
    University Campus, 133 Gill Coliseum, Corvallis, OR 97331
    Behavior modification techniques for parents of handicapped children.

Kris: A Family Portrait. 1975, color, 18 minutes
    Ithaca College Communications Center
    Ithaca, NY 14850
    Relationships of a blind and retarded child to his family.

Language Development. 20 minutes
    CRM Productions
    1104 Camino Del Mar, Del Mar, CA 92014
    Progression from cooing, to babbling, to speech is traced through use
    of animated drawings.

LATON—A Handicapped Child in Need. 1977, color, 14½ minutes
    Campus Film Distributors
    2 Overhill Road, Scarsdale, NY 10583
    Designed to inform and motivate parents of handicapped children eli-
    gible for Head Start to bring their children to the program; discusses
    services provided by Head Start.

LATON—A Head Start Child and His Parents. 1977, color 14½ minutes
   Campus Film Distributors
   2 Overhill Road, Scarsdale, NY 10583
   Focuses on parental involvement in the education and therapy of a
   handicapped child enrolled in Head Start.

Learning. 30 minutes
   CRM Productions
   1104 Camino Del Mar, Del Mar, CA 92014
   Shows a variety of experiments (e.g., behavior shaping, teaching language
   to a mentally retarded child) using principles of operant conditioning.

Learning to Learn in Infancy. B/W, 30 minutes
   Modern Talking Pictures Service
   1212 Avenue of the Americas, New York, NY 10036
   Stresses the essential role of curiosity and exploration in learning and
   points to the kinds of experience that cultivate and stimulate an eager
   approach to the world.

Leo Beuerman. 1969, color, 13 minutes
   Centron Educational Films
   1621 West Ninth Street, Lawrence, KS 66044
   How a man, physically handicapped since birth, overcame adversity; his
   philosophy of life.

Let Me See. 1952, 20 minutes
   University of Southern California, Division of Cinema
   University Park, Los Angeles, CA 90007
   Cooperation and understanding necessary in helping a visually handi-
   capped child.

Like Everybody Else. 1977, color, 32 minutes
   Stanfield House Films
   Box 3208, Santa Monica, CA 90403
   One of the country's largest comprehensive programs for retarded adults,
   the AHRC Vocational Training Center in Freeport, Long Island, is shown
   in this film.

Like Other People. 1973, color, 37 minutes
   Perennial Education
   1825 Willow Road, Northfield, IL 60093
   A narration of the social, emotional, and sexual needs of physically
   handicapped young people.

Mainstreaming in Action. 1979, color, 25 minutes
   Encyclopedia Britannica Educational Corporation
   425 North Michigan Avenue, Chicago, IL 60611
   Discusses concerns regarding placement of handicapped children in the
   least restrictive environment. The film also includes a user's guide.

Mainstreaming Techniques: Life Science and Art. 1980, color, 12 minutes
McGraw-Hill
1221 Avenue of the Americas, New York, NY 10020
Illustrates the involvement activities, interactions, and responses of
blind, deaf, and disturbed children in a mainstreamed life science and
art program.

Martha. 1978, color, 8 minutes
Films, Inc.
733 Green Bay Road, Wilmette, IL 60091
This film demonstrates that persons with epilepsy can lead a full,
active life.

A Matter of Inconvenience. 1974, color, 10 minutes
Stanfield House
12381 Wilshire Boulevard, Suite 203, Los Angeles, CA 90025
How blind and amputee individuals refuse to accept stereotypes. Illustrates the difference between a disability and a handicap.

Michael—A Mongoloid Child. 1961, 14 minutes
New York University, Audio Visual Center
26 Washington Place, New York, NY 10003
A 15-year-old Mongoloid boy is shown with his rural English family,
who have accepted his handicap.

Mimi. 1972, B/W, 12 minutes
Billy Budd Films
235 East 57th Street, New York, NY 10022
A young paralyzed woman's account of her life and how she relates to
others.

The Music Child. 1976, 46 minutes
Benchmark Films, Inc.
145 Scarborough Road, Briarcliff Manor, NY 10510
Presents the possibilities for eliciting language, basic communication,
and relationships with handicapped children through a special type of
music therapy based on "live" musical improvisation.

Nature of Mental Retardation. Color, 32 minutes
University of Kansas
746 Massachusetts Street, Lawrence, KS 66044
Relates vocational counseling to the various adaptive behavior levels of
retarded children. Discusses causes and rehabilitation potential of
different levels.

New Nursery School Series. Color, 25 minutes, 17 minutes, and 18 minutes
    Modern Talking Pictures Service
    1212 Avenue of the Americas, New York, NY 10036
    These three films describe the Responsive Environment Nursery School, an
    intervention program designed to aid poor children in their total devel-
    opment.

Nicky: One of My Best Friends. Color, 15 minutes
    McGraw-Hill
    1221 Avenue of the Americas, New York, NY 10020
    Story of a 10-year-old boy who is blind and has cerebral palsy, and who
    has been mainstreamed.

Non-SLIP. 1975, color, 25 minutes
    University of Kansas, Audio Visual Center
    6 Bailey Hall, Lawrence, KS 66044
    Demonstrates Non Speech Language Initiation Program training procedures
    and gives some background in the area of symbolic language research.

Not Without Hope. 1964, color, 23 minutes
    Marshall Faber
    6412 East Dessert Cove, Scottsdale, AZ 85254
    Problems and obstacles of people with epilepsy.

Not Without Sight. 1973, color, 19 minutes
    American Foundation for the Blind, Public Education Division
    15 West Sixteenth Street, New York, NY 10011
    Identification of common eye disorders such as tunnel vision, retinitis,
    pigmentosa, cataracts.

One Step at a Time: An Introduction to Behavior Modification. 1973, color,
28 minutes
    Contemporary/McGraw-Hill Films, Sales Service Department
    110 15th Street, Del Mar, CA 92014
    Modification of behavior by rewarding desirable traits rather than by
    punishing undesirable ones.

Pancho. Color, 24 minutes
    Modern Talking Pictures Service
    1212 Avenue of the Americas, New York, NY 10036
    The film depicts Pancho, during the course of extensive medical treat-
    ment for hypothyroidism, changing from a listless, apathetic child into
    a happy energetic youngster. Available in Spanish.

Parents Are Teachers, Too. B/W, 22 minutes.
    Modern Talking Pictures Service
    1212 Avenue of the Americas, New York, NY 10036
    The film's school situation presents ideas for parents to use in en-
    couraging a child's mental and emotional growth through play.

Parents of Disturbed Children. 1975, color, 28 minutes
    Stanfield House
    900 Euclid Avenue, P.O. Box 3208, Santa Monica, CA 90403
    Shows how parents have come to accept their child's disturbance.

Peer-Conducted Behavior Modification. 1976, color, 24 minutes
    The Media Guild
    Box 881, Solano Beach, CA 92075
    Role of peers in shaping and reinforcing deviant behavior, and their
    value in a therapy program employing them as positive behavior modi-
    fiers.

People You'd Like to Know. 1978, color, 10 minutes
    Encyclopedia Britannica Educational Corporation
    425 North Michigan Avenue, Chicago, IL 60611
    Helps students, teachers, and others become acquainted with the problems
    of handicapped youths as they become mainstreamed.

Personalized Reading for Children. 1977, color, 30 minutes
    Agency for Instructional Television
    Box a, Bloomington, IN 47402
    Dickerson School in Buena Park, California, organizes in an atmosphere
    of trust and cooperation to design a reading program for individual
    needs.

Person to Person In Infancy. B/W, 22 minutes
    Modern Talking Pictures Service
    1212 Avenue of the Americas, New York, NY 10036
    Film stresses the importance of human relationships between infant and
    adult.

Physical Development. 1980, color, 21 minutes
    CRM, McGraw-Hill
    110 Fifteenth Street, Del Mar, CA 92014
    Overview of normal physical growth from infancy to adolescence, per-
    ceptual-motor skills, and a movement education program for LD and normal
    children.

A Place Among Us. NBC/TV, 1970, color, 22 minutes
     Educational Enterprises
     Rockefeller Plaza, NY 10020
     Describes two programs for the mentally retarded, one research-oriented
     and one vocational, which focus on returning individuals to the com-
     munity.

Portrait of a Disadvantaged Child: Tommy Knight. 1965, 16 minutes
     McGraw-Hill Films, Sales Service Department
     1221 Avenue of the Americas, New York, NY 10020
     Special problems, needs, and strengths of the inner-city child.

Principles of Parent-Child Programs for the Preschool Hearing Impaired.
1967, 28 minutes
     The Pennsylvania State University, Department of Audiovisual Services
     Special Services Building, University Park, PA 16802
     Contrast between the audiological work done with hearing-impaired chil-
     dren and their parents in the usual clinical setting, and the work done
     in an intensive program.

P.L. 94-142: Equality of Opportunity. 1977, color, 21 minutes
     Instructional Media Services
     128 East Pittsburgh Street, Greensburg, PA 15601
     Explanation of the complex legislation in P.L. 94-142, which provides
     for public education of all handicapped children.

Quiet One. 1948, 66 minutes
     McGraw-Hill Films, Sales Service Department
     1221 Avenue of the Americas, New York, NY 10020
     Classic fictional film that shows the ghetto's devastating psychological
     effects.

Readin' and Writin' Ain't Everything. 1975, color, 26 minutes
     Stanfield House
     12381 Wilshire Boulevard, Suite 203, Los Angeles, CA 90025
     The personal accounts of young mentally retarded adults and three
     families with mentally retarded children. It emphasizes the need for
     acceptance and understanding.

Report on Down's Syndrome. 1964, color, 22 minutes
     International Film Bureau
     332 South Michigan Avenue, Chicago, IL 60604
     Comprehensive review of Down's Syndrome.

A School Day: Study of a Visually Handicapped Child. 1969, 24 minutes
    New York University
    26 Washington Place, New York, NY 10003
    Shows that in a supportive atmosphere created by home, school, and
    community, a blind child can develop to his full potential.

Show Me. 1966, 28 minutes
    Universal Education & Visual Arts
    100 University City Plaza, Universal City, CA 91608
    Designed to promote the teaching of movement and rhythm to the mentally
    retarded.

Siblings As Behavior Modifiers. 1975, color, 30 minutes
    The Media Guild
    Box 881, Solano Beach, CA 92075
    Teaches the family new management techniques of behavior modification
    to help them handle a retarded child.

Sit Down, Shut Up or Get Out. 1971, color, 58 minutes
    Films Incorporated
    1144 Wilmette Avenue, Wilmette, IL 60091
    This allegorical play about an intellectually gifted boy with behavior
    problems deals with the threat to individual freedom involved in the
    expression of dissent.

Somebody Waiting. 1972, color, 24 minutes
    University of California, Extension Media Center
    Berkeley, CA 94720
    Effects of appropriate environmental stimulation and therapeutic
    handling of hospitalized children with severe cerebral dysfunction.

Some of Our Schoolmates Are Blind. 1960, color, 20 minutes
    Hollywood Film Enterprises
    6060 Sunset Boulevard, Hollywood, CA 90038
    A public elementary school that includes blind students.

The Sooner the Better. 1979, color, 27 minutes
    Third Eye Films
    12 Arrow Street, Cambridge, MA 02138
    Ideas for preschool teachers for developing nonsexist approaches to
    early childhood education.

Special Children Special Needs. 1978, color, 22 minutes
    Campus Film Distributors
    2 Overhill Road, Scarsdale, NY 10583
    Developmental approach to educating young multihandicapped children in
    three adapted learning environments.

Special Education Placement: Issues and Alternatives. 1976, color
    The Council for Exceptional Children, Publication Sales
    1920 Association Drive, Reston, VA 22091
    Introduces a decision-making system dealing with placements and legal
    considerations: assessment, due process, labeling, and categorizing,
    referral, evaluation and programming, parent involvement, litigation.

Special Education Techniques: Lab Science And Art. 1980, color, 24 minutes
    McGraw-Hill
    1221 Avenue of the Americas, New York, NY 10020
    Shows gifted and average blind children performing science and art
    activities in a self-contained elementary classroom, including special
    adaptations and teaching strategies.

Specific Learning Disabilities in the Classroom. 1975, color, 23 minutes
    Davidson Films, Inc.
    165 Tunstead Avenue, San Anselmo, CA 94960
    Defines and documents the most common types of learning disabilities.

Specific Learning Disabilities: Evaluation. 1975, color, 27 minutes
    Davidson Films, Inc.
    165 Tunstead Avenue, San Anselmo, CA 94960
    Follows two learning-disabled children through a series of evaluative
    tasks to determine their learning strengths and weaknesses, giving
    teachers practical understanding of techniques.

Specific Learning Disabilities: Remedial Programming. 1975, color, 28 minutes
    Davidson Films, Inc.
    165 Tunstead Avenue, San Anselmo, CA 94960
    Describes how information gained through evaluation and observation can
    be translated into appropriate individualized remedial planning.

Step By Step. 1980, color, 14½ minutes
    Campus Film Distributors
    2 Overhill Road, Scarsdale, NY 10583
    Presents a program of mainstreaming preschool children with handicapping
    conditions in a public school based on a prekindergarten program.

Stress: Parents with a Handicapped Child. 1967, 28 minutes
    McGraw-Hill Films, Sales Service Department
    1221 Avenue of the Americas, New York, NY 10020
    The home life of five families with handicapped children.

The Teaching Triad. 1973, color, 17 minutes
    Aims Instructional Media Services, Inc.
    P.O. Box 1010, Hollywood, CA 90028
    Demonstrates ways teachers and parents together can bring the child to
    optimal levels of development.

These People. 1980, color, 29 minutes
>   Perennial Education, Inc.
>   477 Roger Williams, P.O. Box 855 Ravina, Highland Park, IL 60035
>   Case study of the response of private citizens to the development of
>   community care facilities for the mentally ill and the mentally re-
>   tarded in their community.

They Call Me Names. 1972, color, 22 minutes
>   BFA Educational Media
>   211 Michigan Avenue, P.O. Box 1795, Santa Monica, CA 90406
>   How mentally deficient young people perceive the world in which they
>   are told they are "different."

A Time for Georgia. 1971, B/W, 14 minutes
>   New York University Film Library
>   26 Washington Place, New York, NY 10003
>   Documents a 4-year-old autistic child's struggles and triumphs in
>   her classroom world and shows her progress within a 6-month period.

A Time to Learn. 1973, color, 24 minutes
>   Kennedy Center
>   Box 40, Peabody College, Nashville, TN 37203
>   Documentation of the Toddler Research and Intervention Project, focusing
>   on language training, parent participation, and mainstreaming.

The Time Has Come. 1979, color, 22 minutes
>   Third Eye Films
>   12 Arrow Street, Cambridge, MA 02138
>   Nonsexist approaches to parenting; examines what's involved in a non-
>   sexist environment and looks at outside influences such as school and
>   television.

Time's Lost Children. 1973, color, 29 minutes
>   Indiana University, Audio-Visual Center
>   Bloomington, IN 47401
>   Parents, teachers, and doctors examine the private and mysterious world
>   of the autistic child.

Token Economy: Behaviorism Applied. 1972, color, 21 minutes
>   Contemporary/McGraw-Hill Films, Sales Service Department
>   110 15th Street, Del Mar, CA 92014
>   Dr. B. F. Skinner explains the use of "tokens" in a program of rein-
>   forcement therapy, developing his theories of behaviorism and demon-
>   strating their applications in an educational environment.

Training Programs and Techniques. 1970, color, 25 minutes
University of Kansas
746 Massachusetts Street, Lawrence, KS 66044
This film shows three types of training used in rehabilitation programs
for the retarded: a mechanical skills program for educables, sheltered
workshop for trainables, and cottage programs for severely retarded.

Triumph of Christy Brown. 1971, B/W, 60 minutes
Indiana University, Audiovisual Center
Bloomington, IN 47401
An Irish author and painter and the cerebral palsy handicaps he overcame.

Try Another Way. 1975, color, 27 minutes
Film Productions of Indianapolis
128 East 36th Street, Indianapolis, IN 46205
Approach to teaching complex assembly tasks to the mentally retarded,
developed by Dr. Marc Gold at the Children's Research Center, University
of Illinois.

Try Another Way Training Series. 1975, color, 12-22 minutes
Film Productions of Indianapolis
128 East 36th Street, Indianapolis, IN 46205
A series of training films demonstrating Dr. Marc Gold's philosophy and
work with the mentally retarded. The series contains an overview film
and others on task analysis and feedback—all of which illustrate
Gold's educational methods for trainers who work with the retarded.

Understanding the Deaf. 1977, B/W, 21 minutes
Perennial Education, Inc.
477 Roger Williams, P.O. Box 855 Ravina, Highland Park, IL 60035
Film to assist teachers and students in regular public schools to
understand and communicate with deaf and hard-of-hearing children who
enter the regular classroom.

Understanding the Gifted. 1964, 33 minutes
Classroom Films Distributors, Inc.
5610 Hollywood Boulevard, Los Angeles, CA 90028
Knowledge that has been accumulated on the characteristics of the
gifted since the 1920s.

Walk Awhile in My Shoes. 1974, color, 28 minutes
Stanfield House
12381 Wilshire Boulevard, Suite 203, Los Angeles, CA 90025
Problems the disabled must face because of transportation systems and
buildings that are geared for the average person.

War of the Eggs. 1971, B/W or color, 26 minutes
     Insight Films
     P.O. Box 1057, Pacific Palisades, CA 90272
     Exploration of the child-battering syndrome.

What Color Is The Wind? 1973, color, 27 minutes
     Allan Grant Productions
     P.O. Box 49244, Los Angeles, CA 90046
     True story of twin boys, one born blind, and their parents' determina-
     tion to treat both equally.

What Do You Do When You See a Blind Person? 1971, color, 13 minutes
     Rapid Film Technique
     37-02 27th Street, Long Island City, NY 11101
     Right and wrong ways of dealing with blind people in particular
     situations.

Where to Begin With Non-Verbal Children. 1974, color, 17 minutes
     Kansas University Affiliated Facility
     223 Harworth, Lawrence, KS 66045
     Shows one technique for making a gross evaluation of the functional
     behavior of nonverbal children.

Who Are the DeBolts? Color, 27 minutes
     PYRAMID
     Box 1048, Santa Monica, CA 90406
     A documentary about the DeBolt family of 19 children. All but five are
     very special children—handicapped, Korean War orphans, Vietnamese
     War orphans, a blind American boy, a girl born without legs.

Why Can't I Learn? 1975, color, 50 minutes
     Capital Cities Broadcasting Company
     24 East 51st Street, New York, NY 10022
     Dramatizes home, school, and social struggle of a learning disabled
     child; offers hope for recognition and treatment of these children.

You Have Got the Power. 1978, color, 27 minutes
     Stanfield House Films/Media
     12381 Wilshire Boulevard, Suite 203, Los Angeles, CA 90025
     About bone cancer amputees and the rehabilitation process.

Other Media

Filmstrips

Children with Handicaps: What Makes Them Special? 1980, color
    Parents' Magazine Films, Inc.
    Box 1000, Elmsford, NY 10523
    A collection of four sets of filmstrips: Behavioral and Emotional Disabilities, Physical Disabilities, Intellectual Disabilities, and Educational and Language Disabilities. Each set contains five full-color filmstrips, either one LP record or three tape cassettes, five audio script booklets, one discussion guide, and a library processing kit. Guidelines for detecting and treating behavioral, emotional, physical, intellectual, educational, and language disabilities are presented.

The Effective Parent: Teaching a Child to Learn. 1980, color
    Parents' Magazine Films, Inc.
    Box 1000, Elmsford, NY 10523
    A collection of four sets of filmstrips: The Parent as a Teacher, Learning in the Home, Learning Away From Home, and Learning Through Play. Each set contains five full-color filmstrips, one LP record or three tape cassettes, five audio script booklets, one discussion guide, and one library processing kit. This series is designed to give parents, prospective parents, and professionals insights and techniques that will help them prepare young children for learning.

Emotional Impairment in Preschool Children. 1980, color, 10 minutes
    Campus Film Distributors Corp.
    14 Madison Avenue, Valhalla, NY 10595
    This filmstrip illustrates ways to identify the signs of emotional impairments in preschool children and gives suggestions for a caregiver to follow to aid in mainstreaming.

Even Love is Not Enough. 1975, color
    Parents' Magazine Films, Inc.
    Box 1000, Elmsford, NY 10523
    A collection of four sets of filmstrips: Behavioral and Emotional Disabilities, Physical Disabilities, Intellectual Disabilities, and Education and Language Disabilities. Each set contains five full-color filmstrips, either an LP record or cassettes, script book, and a discussion guide.

Hearing Impairments in Preschool Children. 1980, color, 10 minutes
    Campus Film Distributors Corp.
    14 Madison Avenue, Valhalla, NY 10595
    The various kinds of hearing impairments and the factors related to
    causes of conditions are discussed. The ways a caregiver can help the
    child develop through a multisensory approach is also presented.

Kids, Mainstreaming, and You. 1979, color, 16 minutes
    The Kids Come in Special Flavors Company
    Box 562, Forest Park Station, Dayton, OH 45405
    This sound filmstrip uses a cartoon format and nontechnical language
    to communicate the essentials of the mainstreaming process.

Learning Disabilities in Preschool Children. 1980, color, 10 minutes
    Campus Film Distributors Corp.
    14 Madison Avenue, Valhalla, NY 10595
    Filmstrip of commonly observable characteristics of learning disabled
    preschool children (recognizing visual perception and motor coordination
    problems as well as emotional and behavioral problems).

A New Look at the Retarded. Color
    Regional Resource Center
    4400 Franklin Street, Harrisburg, PA 17111
    General introduction to retardation and the adjustment the families
    must make. Five filmstrips and audio cassettes.

Observing Young Children.
    Pinnacle Educational Products
    P.O. Box 867, Auburn, AL 36830
    Five filmstrips and audio cassettes on observing young children includ-
    ing: Introduction, Classroom Environment, Using Materials, Social De-
    velopment, Fine Motor Skill Development.

Parent-Teacher Conferences. 1968, color, 15 minutes
    Foreworks
    Box 9747, North Hollywood, CA 91609
    This filmstrip helps to improve communication between parents and
    teachers.

Physical and Health Impairments in Preschool Children. 1980, color, 10 minutes
    Campus Film Distributors Corp.
    14 Madison Avenue, Valhalla, NY 10595
    The causes and characteristics of ten disorders and their medical desig-
    nations are discussed. Ways of adapting the physical environment, spe-
    cific curriculum, and teaching suggestions to help impaired preschool
    children are presented.

Precision-Teaching. 1976, color, 25 minutes
    Council for Exceptional Children
    1920 Association Drive, Reston, VA   22091
    Introduction to precision teaching, demonstrating key procedures in
    individualizing instruction, motivating students, and evaluating
    teaching efforts.

Special Education. 1980, color
    Parents' Magazine Films, Inc.
    Box 1000, Elmsford, NY   10523
    A collection of four sets of filmstrips: Teacher Training, Meeting
    Mimi, This is Who I Am, and Put Yourself in My Place. Each set contains
    full-color filmstrips, tape cassettes or LP records, a teacher's guide,
    and a library processing kit. This service provides specific suggestions
    for classroom situations to help encourage empathy and acceptance of the
    handicapped.

Speech and Language Inpairment in Preschool Children. 1980, color, 10 minutes
    Campus Film Distributors Corp.
    14 Madison Avenue, Valhalla, NY   10595
    The levels of language development are described. The physical, emotion-
    al, and environmental factors affecting speech are discussed and specif-
    ic ideas for teaching and mainstreaming are presented.

Teacher-Made Games and Activities for Young Children.
    Pinnacle Educational Products
    P.O. Box 867, Auburn, AL   36830
    Filmstrip and audio cassette about 35 teacher-made games and activities
    designed to help preschool and primary-level children develop skills in:
    visual and tactile discrimination, matching, reading, mathematics,
    seriation, classification, fine motor tasks.

Teacher-Made Reading Games and Activities.
    Pinnacle Educational Products
    P.O. Box 867, Auburn, AL   36830
    Filmstrip and audio cassette on 18 teacher-made games and activities
    designed to help elementary children develop skills in: visual dis-
    crimination, word attack, comprehension, content area reading.

Visual Impairments in Preschool Children. 1980, color, 10 minutes
    Campus Film Distributors Corp.
    14 Madison Avenue, Valhalla, NY   10595
    Detection of visual problems in preschool children is discussed along
    with classifications of visual impairments. Suggestions for providing
    a concrete approach to teaching the visually impaired child are also
    presented.

Working With Handicapped Children: A Special Need, A Special Love. 1980, color
   Parents' Magazine Films, Inc.
   Box 1000, Elmsford, NY 10523
   A collection of four sets of filmstrips: Support From the Family, Support
   From Educators, Support From the Helping Professions, and Support From
   the Community. Each set contains five full-color filmstrips, one LP
   record or three tape cassettes, five audio script booklets, one discussion guide, and a library processing kit. This series discusses how
   parents can secure help from other family members, from school systems
   and individual educators, and from professional organizations in their
   communities.

Slides/Tapes/Cassettes

The Autistic Child. 48 minutes
   JAB Press
   P.O. Box 39852, Los Angeles, CA 90039
   Major theories about autistic children are discussed.

The CEC Invisible College Conference on the Severely, Profoundly, and
Multiply Handicapped.
   Council for Exceptional Children
   1920 Association Drive, Reston, VA 22091
   Presentations by noted professionals covering many facets of the
   education and training of this group.

Education: Special for the Mexican American.
   Council for Exceptional Children
   1920 Association Drive, Reston, VA 22091
   Focuses on bilingual education and assessment of bilingual children.

Establishing Characteristics of Children with Learning Disabilities.
   JAB Press
   P.O. Box 39852, Los Angeles, CA 90039
   Characteristics of learning disabled children are discussed.

If You Knew Us Better.
   Council for Exceptional Children
   1920 Association Drive, Reston, VA 22091
   Eight cassettes giving perspectives on education, learning styles, family
   culture, and social values of different cultural groups.

Improving Services: Court Action and Child Advocacy.
   Council for Exceptional Children
   1920 Association Drive, Reston, VA 22091
   Looks at court action and child advocacy model.

Mainstreaming and the Resource Room Model.
    JAB Press
    P.O. Box 39852, Los Angeles, CA   90039
    The resource room model as a vital support system for mainstreaming is
    discussed.

Parents Talk About Mainstreaming.
    LINC Outreach, Eliot-Pearson Children's School
    Tufts University, 105 College Avenue, Medford, MA   02155

Professional Diagnosis.
    Chapel Hill Training—Outreach Program
    Lincoln Center, Chapel Hill, NC   27514

Section 504.
    Chapel Hill Training—Outreach Program
    Lincoln Center, Chapel Hill, NC   27514

Teachers Talk About Mainstreaming.
    LINC Outreach, Eliot-Pearson Children's School
    Tufts University, 105 College Avenue, Medford, MA   02155

They Shall Create: Gifted Minority Children.
    Council for Exceptional Children
    1920 Association Drive, Reston, VA   22091
    Readings and comments on poetry and prose by Black American youth.
    How the Mexican-American community perceives and identifies exceptional
    children.

Where Difference Is Respected. Mainstreaming Special Needs Children in a
Developmentally Oriented Classroom.
    LINC Outreach, Eliot-Pearson Children's School
    Tufts University, 105 College Avenue, Medford, MA   02155

Multimedia

The Culturally Different Learner.
    National Education Association
    1201 Sixteenth Street, N.W., Washington, DC   20036
    Two filmstrips, tapes, and response booklets dealing with the learning
    styles of culturally different learners and the role different types of
    instructional media play in teaching the culturally different.

Everybody Counts! A Workshop Manual to Increase Awareness of Handicapped People.

> Council for Exceptional Children
> 1920 Association Drive, Reston, VA 22091
> Designed as an initial experiential learning strategy to assist groups toward a fuller understanding of the needs and desires of disabled individuals. The kit includes suggested materials, handouts, discussion guide, and a tape cassette.

Foster Parenting a Retarded Child.

> Foster Parent Curriculum Project, Child Welfare League of America
> 67 Irving Place, New York, NY 10003
> Curriculum to increase skills and sensitivity in caring for retarded children. The package consists of films, tapes, workbooks, a leader's manual, and supplementary readings.

Good Start! A Multimedia Approach to Meeting the Needs of Visually Handicapped Students.

> American Foundation for the Blind, Inc.; Attention: Film Librarian
> 15 West 16th Street, New York, NY 10011
> This kit consists of: one 16 mm film, color, 19 minutes; six filmstrips, color, 12 minutes each; and supplementary materials. It is designed for all persons involved in the mainstreaming of visually impaired children.

Hi-Fi.

> National Audiovisual Center, General Services Administration
> Washington, DC 20409
> This kit consists of a teacher's manual, 7-minute audio cassette, 12-minute black and white videotape, and 32 transparency masters. It is designed as a special education in-service workshop to teach the public school teacher the needs and characteristics of hearing impaired children.

How Can Tests Be Unfair? A Workshop on Nondiscriminatory Testing.

> Council for Exceptional Children
> 1920 Association Drive, Reston VA 22091
> Six simulation activities to allow participants to experience test biases encountered by children with different language or cultural backgrounds. Kit includes directions to the leader and booklets for participants.

I Am, I Can, I Will.

> Hubbard
> P.O. Box 104, Northbrook, IL 60062
> 16 mm film, audio cassettes, videotapes, and books. Mister Roger's program designed to help young children and their friends with handicaps to understand feelings.

An Introductory Course in Learning Disabilities.
>   Book-Lab, Inc.
>   1449 Thirty-Seventh Street, Brooklyn, NY 11218
>   This kit consists of one cassette for each session: Psycho-Educational
>   battery, Glossary of Learning Disabilities, Guidelines to Teaching Re-
>   medial Reading, Issues in Urban Education and Mental Health, and the
>   study guide. This kit is an in-service/preservice training program that
>   provides a conceptual and practical orientation to the field of learning
>   disabilities.

Preparing for the IEP Meeting: A Workshop for Parents.
>   Council for Exceptional Children
>   1920 Association Drive, Reston, VA 22091
>   Two-hour training package designed to help parents become productive
>   participants of the IEP conference. The kit includes reproducible mate-
>   rials, IEP evaluation checklists, a filmstrip, and leader's guide.

Project Mainstream.
>   Educational Progress Corporation
>   Tulsa, OK
>   Audiotape cassettes, activity sheets, and teacher's guide designed to
>   present pupils with learning and behavioral disabilities in preschool
>   through grade 3 with activities intended to develop skills in auditory,
>   visual, and social/emotional behaviors.

P.L. 94-142: The Education for All Handicapped Children Act of 1975.
>   Council for Exceptional Children
>   1920 Association Drive, Reston, VA 22091
>   Developed to help educators and parents understand the many facets of
>   P.L. 94-142. Kit includes three captioned films and audio cassettes, a
>   copy of the law, and a question and answer document.

P.L. 94-142: Implementing Procedural Safeguards—A Guide for Schools and
Parents.
>   Council for Exceptional Children
>   1920 Association Drive, Reston, VA 22091
>   Focuses on due process regarding the rights and protection of educators,
>   parents, and children; includes filmstrips, cassettes, discussion guide,
>   and dittomasters.

Special Delivery.
>   Lawren Publications, Inc.
>   P.O. Box 666, Mendocino, CA 95460
>   This kit consists of five videotapes, and a package of printed materials
>   including the teacher's handbook. The film is designed to help children
>   develop a more positive attitude and understanding towards handicapped
>   peers.

Special Education Placement: Issues and Alternatives—A Decision Making Module.
>   Council for Exceptional Children
>   1920 Association Drive, Reston, VA 22091
>   Complete course package for preservice and in-service training that includes a 16 mm film, self-instructive, self-pacing units, and modules.

Special Needs In-Service Programs.
>   ESN Press
>   85 Main Street, Watertown, MA 02172
>   Seven program packages of practical help for teachers on what to do about special learners. Kits include books, practical ideas, case studies, resources, filmstrips, and cassette tapes.

Systematic Training for Effective Parenting.
>   American Guidance Service
>   Publishers' Building, Circle Pines, MN 55014
>   The kit includes an introductory cassette, invitational brochures, an announcement poster, a leader's manual, a parent's handbook, instructional cassettes, discussion guide cards, posters, and charts. The program is for parents and others who want to develop more satisfying relationships with children.

Video Training Workshops on Child Variance.
>   Council for Exceptional Children, Publication Sales
>   1920 Association Drive, Reston, VA 22091
>   This kit contains six video cassettes, a workshop leader's manual, student text with six self-instructional modules, and activity sheets. This kit is designed to help teachers, parents, and paraprofessionals understand variant behaviors among children, and to better accept and relate to children with behavior problems.

We Can Help.
>   Council for Exceptional Children
>   1920 Association Drive, Reston, VA 22091
>   A specialized curriculum for educators on the prevention and treatment of child abuse and neglect that includes trainer's guides, overhead transparencies, and filmstrips.

What If You Couldn't . . .?
>   Selective Educational Equipment, Inc.
>   3 Bridge Street, P.O. Box 98, Newton, MA 02195
>   This kit consists of an evaluation package and a set of seven teacher's guides. It is designed to present children with a nonthreatening, straightforward picture of what it might be like to have a disability.

Workshop: Creating Instructional Materials for Handicapped Learners.
     National Audiovisual Center
     General Services Administration, Washington, DC 20409
     This set consists of three audio cassettes, two color filmstrips, and
     a coordinator's guide. The workshop shows teachers how to create mate-
     rials for handicapped learners and offers guidelines in the selection,
     evaluation, adaptation, and use of commercial materials.

Books of Special Interest to Teachers

Abeson, A. R., Bolick, N., and Hass, J. A Primer on Due Process—Education Decisions for Handicapped Children. Reston, Va.: Council for Exceptional Children, 1975.

Abidin, R. R. Parenting Skills: Trainer's Manual and Workbook. New York: Human Sciences Press, 1976.

Adams, D., Crandall, A., Eckhoff, B., and Woods-Elliot, C. Sparks for Learning: Ideas for Teaching Reading and Language Arts. Watertown, Mass.: ESN Press, 1980.

Adkins, P. G. A Priceless Playground for Exceptional Children. El Paso, Tex.: Early Learning Center for Exceptional Children, 1973.

Ainscow, M., and Tweddle, D. A. Preventing Classroom Failure: An Objective Approach. New York: Wiley, 1979.

Alley, G. A., and Deshler, D. D. Teaching the Learning Disabled Adolescent: Strategies and Methods. Denver, Col.: Love Publishing, 1979.

Almy, M., and Genishi, C. Ways of Studying Children: An Observational Manual for Early Childhood Teachers. New York: Teachers College Press, 1979.

Anderson, R. Individualizing Educational Materials for Special Children in the Mainstream. Baltimore: University Park Press, 1978.

Auerbach, S. A. Creative Homes and Centers. New York: Human Sciences Press, 1978.

Auerbach, S. Special Needs and Services. New York: Human Sciences Press, 1979.

Axelrod, S. Behavior Modification for the Classroom Teacher. New York: McGraw-Hill, 1977.

Banas, N., and Wills, I. H. Identifying Early Learning Gaps: A Guide to the Assessment of Academic Readiness. Atlanta, Ga.: Humanics, 1975.

Baskin, B. H., and Harris, K. H. Books for the Gifted Child. New York: Bowker, 1979.

Baskin, B. H., and Harris, K. H. Notes from a Different Drummer: A Guide to Juvenile Fiction Portraying the Handicapped. New York: Bowker, 1977.

Bateman, B. So You're Going to Hearing. Northbrook, Ill.: Hubbard, 1979.

Behavior Management Strategies for the Classroom. Philadelphia: Research for Better Schools, 1979.

Bender, M. and Valletutti, P. J. Teaching the Moderately and Severely Handicapped—Vol. I: Behavior, Self-care, and Motor Skills; Vol. II: Communication, Socialization, Safety, and Leisure Skills; Vol. III: Functional Academics for the Mildly and Moderately Handicapped. Baltimore: University Park Press, 1976.

Bender, M. and Bender, R. K. Disadvantaged Preschool Children: A Source Book for Teachers. Baltimore: Paul H. Brooks, 1979.

Beter, T. R., and Cragin, W. E. The Mentally Retarded Child and His Motor Behavior: Practical Diagnosis and Movement Experiences. Springfield, Ill.: Charles C. Thomas, 1972.

Birch, J. W. Hearing Impaired Children in the Mainstream. Reston, Va.: Council for Exceptional Children, 1975.

Birch, J. W. Mainstreaming: Educable Mentally Retarded Children in Regular Classes. Reston, Va.: Council for Exceptional Children, 1974.

Blackwell, R. B., and Joynt, R. R. (eds.) Learning Disabilities Handbook for Teachers. Springfield, Ill.: Charles C. Thomas, 1976.

Blumenfeld, J. et al. Help Them Grow! Nashville, Tenn.: Abingdon Press, 1971.

Brolin, D. E. (ed.) Life Centered Career Education—A Competency Based Approach. Reston, Va.: Council for Exceptional Children, 1978.

Brown, D. Behavior Modification in Child, School, and Family Mental Health. Champaign, Ill.: Research Press Company, 1972.

Burgdorf, R. L., Jr. (ed.) The Legal Rights of Handicapped Persons—Cases, Materials, and Text. Baltimore: Paul H. Brooks, 1979.

Caldwell, B. M., and Stedman, D. J., eds. Infant Education: A Guide for Helping Handicapped Children in the First Three Years. New York: Walker and Co., 1977.

Calhoun, M. Teaching and Learning Strategies for Physically Handicapped Students. Baltimore: University Park Press, 1979.

California State Department of Health. Leisure Time Activities for Deaf-Blind Children. Northridge, Calif.: Joyce Media, (no date).

Callahan, C. M. Developing Creativity in the Gifted and Talented. Reston, Va.: Council for Exceptional Children, 1978.

Carlson, B. W., and Ginglend, D. Play Activities for the Retarded Child. Nashville, Tenn.: Abingdon Press, 1971.

Carter, R. D. Help! These Kids Are Driving Me Crazy. Champaign, Ill.: Research Press, 1972.

Cartwright, C. A., and Cartwright, G. P. Developing Observation Skills. New York: McGraw-Hill, 1974.

Cartwright, C., and Forsberg, S. Exceptional Previews: A Self-evaluation Handbook for Special Education Students. Belmont, Calif.: Wadsworth, 1979.

Clarification of P.L. 94-142 for the Classroom Teacher. Philadelphia: Research for Better Schools, 1979.

Clark, G. M. Career Education for the Handicapped Child in the Elementary Classroom. Denver, Col.: Love Publishing, 1979.

Cohen, M. A., and Gross, P. J. The Developmental Resource: Behavioral Sequences for Assessment and Program Planning: Vols. 1 and 2. New York: Grune & Stratton, 1979.

Coletta, A. J. Working Together: A Guide to Parent Involvement. Atlanta, Ga.: Humanics, 1976.

Communications Carousel. Chatsworth, Calif.: Opportunities for Learning, 1977.

Connor, F. P., Williamson, G. G., and Siepp, J. M. Program Guide for Infants and Toddlers with Neuromotor and Other Developmental Disabilities. New York: Teachers College Press, Columbia University, 1978.

Cook, J. E., and Earlley, E. C. Remediating Reading Disabilities: Simple Things That Work. Germantown, Md.: Aspen Systems Corporation, 1979.

Council for Exceptional Children. Career Education: Teaching Exceptional Children. Reston, Va.: Council for Exceptional Children, 1973.

Council for Exceptional Children. Teacher Idea Exchange: A Potpourri of Helpful Hints. Reston, Va.: Council for Exceptional Children, (no date)

Cratty, B. J. Adapted Physical Education for Handicapped Children and Youth. Denver, Col.: Love Publishing, 1980

Cratty, B. J. Developmental Games for Physically Handicapped Children. Palo Alto, Calif.: Peek Publications, 1969.

Cratty, B., and Breen, J. Educational Games for Physically Handicapped Children. Denver, Col.: Love Publishing, 1972.

Cross, L., and Goin, K., eds. Identifying Handicapped Children: A Guide to Casefinding, Screening, Diagnosis, Assessment, and Evaluation. New York: Walker and Co., 1977.

Dayan, M., Harper, B., Malloy, J. S., and Witt, B. T. Communication for the Severely and Profoundly Handicapped. Denver, Col.: Love Publishing, 1975.

Dibner, S. S., and Dibner, A. S. Integration or Segregation for the Physically Handicapped Child. Baltimore: Paul H. Brooks, 1979.

Dorward, B. Teaching Aids and Toys for Handicapped Children. Reston, Va.: Council for Exceptional Children, 1960.

ECE: A Workbook for Administrators, Parents and Volunteers in the Classroom: A Handbook for Teachers. Saratoga, Calif.: R. E. Research Association.

Edgington, D. The Physically Handicapped Child in Your Classroom: A Handbook for Teachers. Springfield, Ill.: Charles C. Thomas, 1976.

Eissler, R. S., Freud, A., Kris, M., and Solnit, A. J., eds. Physical Illness and Handicap in Childhood. New Haven, Conn.: Yale University Press, 1977.

Evans, T. Working with Parents of Handicapped Children. Reston, Va.: Council for Exceptional Children, 1976.

Faas, L. A. Children with Learning Problems: A Handbook for Teachers. Boston: Houghton Mifflin, 1980.

Faas, L. A. Learning Disabilities: A Competency-based Approach. Boston: Houghton Mifflin, 1976.

Feingold, B. A., and Bank, C. L. Developmental Disabilities of Early Childhood. Springfield, Ill.: Charles C. Thomas, 1977.

Filter, M. D. Communication Disorders: A Handbook for Educators. Springfield, Ill.: Charles C. Thomas, 1977.

Fink, A. H. International Perspectives on Future Special Education. Reston, Va.: The Council for Exceptional Children, 1979.

Fraser, B. Gross Motor Management. Vol. II: A Gross Motor Curriculum for Severely and Multiply Impaired Students. Baltimore: University Park Press, 1979.

French, A. Disturbed Children and Their Families: Innovations in Evaluation and Treatment. New York: Human Sciences Press, 1977.

Friedlander, B. Z. Exceptional Infant. Vol. 3: Assessment and Intervention. New York: Brunner/Mazel, 1975.

Gadow, K. D. Children on Medication: A Primer for School Personnel. Reston, Va.: Council for Exceptional Children, 1979.

Gallagher, J. J. "Organizational Needs for Quality Special Education." In Futures of Education for Exceptional Children: Emerging Structures. Minneapolis: University of Minnesota Press, 1978.

Gallagher, P. A. Education Games for Visually Handicapped Children. Denver, Col.: Love Publishing, 1977.

Gallagher, P. A. Positive Classroom Performance: Techniques for Changing Behavior. Denver, Col.: Love Publishing, 1971.

Gallagher, P. A. Teaching Students with Behavior Disorders. Denver, Col.: Love Publishing, 1979.

Gallender, D. Teaching Eating and Toileting Skills to the Multi-handicapped in the School Setting. Springfield, Ill.: Charles C. Thomas, 1979.

Garwood, S. G. Educating Young Handicapped Children: A Developmental Approach. Germantown, Md.: Aspen Systems Corporation, 1979.

Gearhart, B. R., and Willenberg, E. P. Application of Pupil Assessment Information. 3d ed. Denver, Col.: Love Publishing, 1979.

Gordon, I. J., and Breivogel, W. F., eds. Building Effective Home/School Relationships. Rockleish, N.J.: Allyn and Bacon, 1978.

Gregg, E., and Boston Children's Medical Center Staff. What to Do When There's Nothing to Do. Pinebrook, N.J.: Dell Publishing, 1970.

Griswold, V. T., and Starke, T. Multi-cultural Art Projects. Denver, Col.: Love Publishing, 1980.

Grzynkowicz, W. Basic Education for Children with Learning Disabilities. Springfield, Ill.: Charles C. Thomas, 1979.

Guralnick, M. J., ed. Early Intervention and the Integration of Handicapped and Non-handicapped Children. Baltimore: University Park Press, 1978.

Hackett, L. Movement Exploration and Games for the Mentally Retarded. Palo Alto, Calif.: Peek Publications, 1970.

Haring, N. G. Special Education for the Severely Handicapped: The State of the Art in 1975. Reston, Va.: Council for Exceptional Children, 1976.

Haring, N. G., and Schiefelbusch, R. L., eds. Teaching Special Children. New York: McGraw-Hill, 1976.

Hart, V. Beginning with the Handicapped. Springfield, Ill.: Charles C. Thomas, 1974.

Hayes, R. P., and Stevenson, M. G. Teaching the Emotionally Disturbed/Learning Disabled Child: A Practical Guide. Vol. I: Developing Behavior, Instruction and Affective Programs; Vol. II: Assessment for Instruction; Vol. III: Teacher Made Ready-to-use Learning Activities and Games; Vol. IV: Public Law 94-142: A Practical Guide for Teachers, Administrators, and Parents. Washington, D.C.: Acropolis Books Ltd., 1979.

Heasley, B. E., and Grosklos, J. R. Programmed Lessons for Young Language-Disabled Children: A Handbook for Therapists, Educators, and Parents. Springfield, Ill.: Charles C. Thomas, 1976.

Hebeler, J. R., and Reynolds, M. C. Guidelines for Personnel in the Education of Exceptional Children. Reston, Va.: Council for Exceptional Children, 1976.

Helping the Handicapped Through Parent/Professional Partnerships. Niles, Ill.: Developmental Learning Materials, 1979.

Hennon, M. L. Identifying Handicapped Children for Child Development Programs: A Recruitment and Selection Manual. Atlanta, Ga.: Humanics Ltd., 1974.

Heward, W., Dardig, J., and Rossett, A. Working with Parents of Handicapped Children. Columbus, Ohio: Charles E. Merrill, 1979.

Hirst, C. C., and Michaels, E. Developmental Activities for Children in Special Education. Springfield, Ill.: Charles C. Thomas, 1972.

Honig, A. S. Parent Involvement in Early Childhood Education. Rev. ed. Washington, D.C.: NAEYC, 1979.

Hopkins, C. D., and Antes, R. L. Classroom Testing: Administration, Scoring, and Score Interpretation. Itasca, Ill.: Peacock Publishers, 1979.

Irwin, D. M., and Bushnell, M. M. Observational Strategies for Child Study. New York: Holt, Rinehart, and Winston, 1980.

Johnson, N., Jens, K. G., Anderson, J. D., and Gallagher, R. J. "Cognition and Affect in Infancy: Implication for the Handicapped." In New Directions in Special Education. San Francisco, Calif.: Jossey-Bass, 1981.

Jones, M. V. Special Education Programs Within the United States. Springfield, Ill.: Charles C. Thomas, 1968.

Jones, R. L., ed. Mainstreaming and the Minority Child. Reston, Va.: Council for Exceptional Children, 1976.

Jordan, J. B. Exceptional Child Education at the Bicentennial: A Parade of Progress. Reston, Va.: Council for Exceptional Children, 1976-1977.

Jordan, J. B. Teacher Please Don't Close the Door—The Exceptional Child in the Mainstream. Reston, Va.: Council for Exceptional Children, 1976.

Jordan, J. B., Hayden, A. H., and Wood, M., eds. Early Childhood Education for Exceptional Children: A Handbook of Ideas and Exemplary Practices. Reston, Va.: Council for Exceptional Children, 1972.

Jordan, J. B., and Robbins, L. S., eds. Let's Try Doing Something Else Kind of Thing—Behavioral Principles and the Exceptional Child. Reston, Va.: Council for Exceptional Children, 1972.

Kaplan, P., Kohfeldt, T., and Sturla, K. It's Positively Fun: Techniques for Managing Learning Environments. Denver, Col.: Love Publishing, 1974.

Kaplan, S. Providing Programs for the Gifted & Talented—A Handbook. Reston, Va.: Council for Exceptional Children, 1975.

Karnes, M. B. Creative Art for Learning. Reston, Va.: Council for Exceptional Children, 1979.

Karnes, M. B. Creative Games for Learning. Reston, Va.: Council for Exceptional Children, 1977.

Karnes, M. B. Early Childhood. Reston, Va.: Council for Exceptional Children, 1978.

Karnes, M. B. Helping Young Children Develop Language Skills: A Book of Activities. Reston, Va.: Council for Exceptional Children, 1973.

Kelly, L. J. A Dictionary of Exceptional Children. New York: MSS Educational Publishing Co., 1972.

Kent, L. R. Language Acquisition Program for the Retarded or Multiply Impaired. Champaign, Ill.: Research Press, 1974.

Kent, L. R. Language Acquisition Programs for the Severely Retarded. Champaign, Ill.: Research Press, 1974.

Kirk, S. A., Kleibhan, J. M., and Learner, J. W. Teaching Reading to Slow and Disabled Learners. Boston: Houghton Mifflin, 1978.

Kirk, S. A., and Lord, F. E., eds. Exceptional Children: Educational Resources and Perspectives. Boston: Houghton Mifflin, 1974.

Kline, T. Children Move to Learn. Tucson, Ariz.: Communication Skill Builders, 1977.

Koocher, G. P., ed. Children's Rights and the Mental Health Professions. Somerset, N.J.: John Wiley & Sons, 1976.

Kozloff, M. A. Reaching the Autistic Child: A Parent Training Program. Champaign, Ill.: Research Press, 1973.

Krone, A. Art Instruction for Handicapped Children. Denver, Col.: Love Publishing, 1978.

Kroth, R. L. Communicating with Parents of Exceptional Children—Improving Parent-Teacher Relationships. Denver, Col.: Love Publishing, 1977.

Kroth, R. L., and Scholl, G. T. Getting Schools Involved with Parents. Reston, Va.: Council for Exceptional Children, 1978.

Kroth, R. L., and Simpson, R. L. Parent Conferences as a Teaching Strategy. Denver, Col.: Love Publishing, 1977.

Krumboltz, J., and Krumboltz, H. Changing Children's Behavior. Englewood Cliffs, N.J.: Prentice-Hall, 1972.

Larrivee, B. Behavior Management Strategies for Classroom Application: An Inservice Training Manual for Use with Classroom Teachers. Philadelphia: Research for Better Schools, 1979.

Larsen, S. C., and Poplin, M. S. Methods for Educating the Handicapped: An Individualized Education Program Approach. Rockleigh, N.J.: Allyn and Bacon, 1980.

Laslett, R. Educating Maladjusted Children. Denver, Col.: Love Publishing, 1978.

Lerner, J. W., Dawson, D. K., and Horvath, L. T. Cases in Learning and Behavior Problems: A Guide to Individualized Education Programs. Boston: Houghton Mifflin, 1979.

Lillie, D. L. Teaching Parents to Teach: Education for the Handicapped. New York: Walker and Co., 1976.

Linde, T. F., and Kopp, T. Training Retarded Babies and Preschoolers. Springfield, Ill.: Charles C. Thomas, 1974.

Lindsay, Z. Art and the Handicapped Child. New York: Van Nostrand Reinhold, 1972.

Long, K. Johnny's Such a Bright Boy, What a Shame He's Retarded. Boston: Houghton Mifflin, 1977.

Love, H. D., Mainord, J. C., and Naylor, D. Language Development of Exceptional Children. Springfield, Ill.: Charles C. Thomas, 1977.

Lovitt, T. C. Managing Inappropriate Behaviors in the Classroom. Reston, Va.: Council for Exceptional Children, 1978.

Lowell, E. L. Play Is by Ear. Los Angeles, Calif.: John Tracy Clinic, 1963.

Magrab, P. R., and Elder, J. O. Planning for Services to Handicapped Persons: Community, Education, Health. Baltimore: Paul H. Brooks, 1979.

Mann, L., Goodman, L., and Wiederholt, J. L. Teaching the Learning Disabled Adolescent. Boston: Houghton Mifflin, 1977.

Markel, G., and Greenbaum, J. L. Parents Are to Be Seen and Heard: Assertiveness in Educational Planning for Handicapped Children. San Luis Obispo, Calif.: Impact Publishers, 1979.

Martin, G. J., and Hoben, M., eds. Supporting Visually Impaired Students in the Mainstream: The State of the Art. Reston, Va.: Council for Exceptional Children, 1977.

Martin, H. P., ed. The Abused Child: A Multidisciplinary Approach to Developmental Issues and Treatment. Cambridge, Mass.: Ballinger, 1976.

Mather, J. Learning Can Be Child's Play: How Parents Can Help Slower-Than-Average Preschool Children Learn and Develop Through Play Experiences. Nashville, Tenn.: Abingdon Press, 1976.

Mazyck, A. Suggested Equipment and Supplies for Infant-Toddler Centers. Greensboro: North Carolina University, 1969.

McCollum, A. T. Coping with Prolonged Health Impairment in Your Child. Boston: Little, Brown, 1975.

McElderry, T., and Escobedo, L. Tools for Learning—Activities for Young Children with Special Needs. Denver, Col.: Love Publishing, 1980.

McLean, J., and Yoder, D. E., eds. Language Intervention with the Retarded. Baltimore: University Park Press, 1972.

McMurrain, T. T., ed. Orientation to Preschool Assessment. Atlanta, Ga.:
    Humanics, 1979.

Meisels, S. J. Developmental Screening in Early Childhood: A Guide. Wash-
    ington, D.C.: National Association for the Education of Young Children,
    1978.

Merkin, P., and Deno, D., eds. Data Based Program Modification. Reston, Va.:
    Council for Exceptional Children, 1977.

Meyen, E. L., Vergason, G. A., and Whelan, R. J. Alternatives for Teaching
    Exceptional Children. Denver, Col.: Love Publishing, 1977.

Model Vision Project. Chicago, Ill.: Stollting Company, 1980.

Moffett, J., and Wagner, B. J. Student-centered Language Arts and Reading.
    K-13: A Handbook for Teachers. (2nd ed.) Boston: Houghton Mifflin, 1976.

Moran, M. R. Assessment of the Exceptional Learner in the Regular Classroom.
    Denver, Col.: Love Publishing, 1979.

Mullins, J. B. A Teacher's Guide to Management of Physically Handicapped
    Students. Springfield, Ill.: Charles C. Thomas, 1979.

Neisworth, J. T., and Smith, R. M. Modifying Retarded Behavior. Boston:
    Houghton Mifflin, 1973.

Neisworth, J. T., Willoughby-Herb, S., Bagnato, S., Cartwright, C., and
    Laub, K. Individualized Education for Preschool Exceptional Children.
    Germantown, Md.: Aspen Systems Corporation, 1980.

Noland, R. L. Counseling Parents of the Mentally Retarded: A Sourcebook.
    Springfield, Ill.: Charles C. Thomas, 1978.

O'Quinn, G., Jr. Developmental Gymnastics: Building Physical Skills for
    Children. Austin, Tex.: University of Texas, 1979.

Orem, R. C., ed. Montessori and the Special Child. New York: Paragon, 1970.

Otto, W., and Smith, R. J. Corrective and Remedial Teaching. Boston:
    Houghton Mifflin, 1973.

Parker, C. A., ed. Psychological Consultation: Helping Teachers Meet
    Special Needs. Reston, Va.: The Council for Exceptional Children, 1975.

Patterson, G. R. Living with Children: New Methods for Parents and Teachers.
    Champaign, Ill.: Research Press, 1976.

Peck, J. <u>Young Children's Behavior; Implementing Your Goals</u>. Atlanta, Ga.: Humanics, 1978.

Pelosi, J., and Wiegerink, R. "Educational Planning." In <u>Planning for Services to the Handicapped: Community, Education, Health</u>. Baltimore: Paul H. Brooks, in press.

<u>People You'd Like to Know</u>. Chicago: Encyclopedia Britannica Educational Corporation, 1979.

Peter, L. J. <u>Prescriptive Teaching</u>. New York: McGraw-Hill, 1965.

Piazzo, R., and Rothman, R. <u>Preschool Education for the Handicapped</u>. Guilford, Conn.: Special Learning Corporation, 1979.

<u>Precision Teaching: Teaching Exceptional Children</u> (Vol. 3). Reston, Va.: Council for Exceptional Children, 1971.

<u>Progress by Partners in Step, Special Issue on IEP: Teaching Exceptional Children</u> (Vol. 10). Reston, Va.: Council for Exceptional Children, 1978.

Reichard, C. L., and Blackburn, D. B. <u>Music Based Instruction for the Exceptional Child</u>. Denver, Col.: Love Publishing, 1973.

Roger, R. <u>Preschool Programming of Children with Disabilities</u>. Springfield, Ill.: Charles C. Thomas, 1974.

Ross, A. O. <u>The Exceptional Child in the Family—Helping Parents of Exceptional Children</u>. New York: Grune & Stratton, 1964.

Rumanoff, L. A., <u>Curriculum Model for Individuals with Severe Learning and Behavior Disorders</u>. Baltimore: University Park Press, 1979.

Safford, P. L., and Arbitman, D. C. <u>Developmental Intervention with Young Physically Handicapped Children</u>. Springfield, Ill.: Charles C. Thomas, 1975.

Salvia, J., and Ysseldyke, J. <u>Assessment in Special and Remedial Education</u>. Boston: Houghton Mifflin, 1978.

Schattner, R. <u>Early Childhood Curriculum for Multiply Handicapped Children</u>. New York: T. Y. Crowell, 1971.

Schiefelbusch, R. <u>Language Intervention Strategies</u>. Baltimore: University Park Press, 1978.

Schiefelbusch, R. <u>Language Perspectives—Acquisition, Retardation, and Intervention</u>. Baltimore: University Park Press, 1974.

Schifani, J. _Implementing Learning in the Least Restrictive Environment_. Baltimore: University Park Press, 1980.

Schopler, E. _Teaching Strategies for Parents and Professionals_. Baltimore: University Park Press, 1979.

Seaver, J. W., Cartwright, C. A., Ward, C. B., and Heasley, C. A. _Careers with Young Children: Making Your Decision_. Washington, D.C.: National Association for the Education of Young Children, 1979.

Seligman, M. _Strategies for Helping Parents of Exceptional Children: A Guide for Teachers_. Riverside, N.J.: Free Press, 1979.

Siegel, E. _Special Education in the Regular Classroom_. New York: John Day, 1969.

Sponseller, D., ed. _Play as a Learning Medium_. Washington, D.C.: National Association for the Education of Young Children, 1974.

Stabenow, T., and Cratty, B. L. _Speech and Language Problems in Children: A Guide for Parents and Teachers_. Denver, Col.: Love Publishing, 1978.

Stanley, J. C., ed. _Preschool Programs for the Disadvantaged: Five Experimental Approaches to Early Childhood Education_. Baltimore: John Hopkins University Press, 1972.

Stone, J. G. _A Guide to Discipline_. Washington, D.C.: National Association for the Education of Young Children, 1978.

Stott, D. H. _The Hard-to-teach Child: A Diagnostic-Remedial Approach_. Baltimore: University Park Press, 1977.

Suarez, T. M., and Vandivier, P. _Planning for Evaluation—A Resource Book for Programs for Preschool Handicapped Children: Documentation_. Chapel Hill, N.C.: Technical Assistance Development System, 1978.

Swick, K. T., and Duff, E. _Building a Successful Parent/Teacher Partnership_. Atlanta, Ga.: Humanics, 1980.

Thiagarajan, S. et al. _Instructional Development for Training Teachers of Exceptional Children: A Source Book_. Reston, Va.: The Council for Exceptional Children, 1974.

Thomas, M. A., ed. _Hey Don't Forget About Me! Education's Investment in the Severely, Profoundly, and Multiply Handicapped_. Reston, Va.: Council for Exceptional Children, 1976.

Thomas, M. A., ed. Very Special Children Series: Developing Skills in Severely and Profoundly Handicapped Children. Reston, Va.: Council for Exceptional Children, 1977.

Thorum, A. R., Sterns, E. C. et al. Instructional Materials for the Handicapped: Birth Through Early Childhood. Salt Lake City, Utah: Olympus Publishing, 1976.

Toilet Training: Help for the Delayed Learner. New York: McGraw-Hill, 1977.

Turnbull, A. P. "Parent-Professional Interactions." In M. E. Snell, ed. Systematic Instruction for the Moderately and Severely Handicapped. Columbus, Ohio: Charles E. Merrill, 1978.

Turnbull, A. P., and Schulz, J. B. Mainstreaming Handicapped Students: A Guide to Classroom Teachers. Boston: Allyn and Bacon, 1978.

Turnbull, A. P., Strickland, B. B., and Brantley, J. C. Developing and Implementing Individualized Education Programs. Columbus, Ohio: Charles E. Merrill, 1978.

Turnbull, H. R., and Turnbull, A. P. Free Appropriate Public Education: Law and Implementation. Denver, Col.: Love Publishing, 1979.

Van Allen, R. Language Experience Activities. Boston: Houghton Mifflin, 1976.

Van Etten, C. Directory of Selected Instructional Materials. Reston, Va.: Council for Exceptional Children, 1974.

Wabash Center for the Mentally Retarded. Guide for Early Developmental Training. Boston: Allyn and Bacon, 1977.

Walker, H. M. The Acting-out Child: Dealing with Classroom Disruption. Rockleigh, N.J.: Allyn and Bacon, 1979.

Walker, S., 3rd. Help for the Hyperactive Child. Boston: Houghton Mifflin, 1978.

Wallace, G., and Larsen, S. C. Educational Assessment of Learning Problems: Testing for Teaching. Rockleigh, N.J.: Allyn and Bacon, 1978.

Watson, L. S., Jr. Child Behavior Modification: A Manual for Teachers, Nurses, and Parents. Elmsford, N.Y.: British Book Center, 1973.

Webster, E. J. Professional Approaches with Parents of Handicapped Children. Springfield, Ill.: Charles C. Thomas, 1976.

Wedeneyer, A., and Cejyka, T. Creative Ideas for Teaching Exceptional Children. Denver, Col.: Love Publishing, 1975.

Wedeneyer, A., and Cejyka, T. Learning Games for Exceptional Children. Denver, Col.: Love Publishing, 1971.

Wehman, P. Recreation Programming for Developmentally Disabled Persons. Baltimore: University Park Press, 1978.

Wehman, P. Vocational Curriculum for Developmentally Disabled Persons. Baltimore, Md.: University Park Press, 1979.

Weintraub, F. J., Abeson, A. R., Ballard, J., and Lavor, M. L., eds. Public Policy and the Education of Exceptional Children. Reston, Va.: The Council for Exceptional Children, 1976.

Weinberg, R. A., and Wood, F. H., eds. Observation of Pupils and Teachers in Mainstream and Special Education Settings: Alternative Strategies. Reston, Va.: The Council for Exceptional Children, 1975.

Westman, J. C. Child Advocacy. Riverside, N.J.: Free Press, 1979.

Wiederholt, J. L., and Hammill, D. D. The Resource Teacher: A Guide to Effective Practices. Rockleigh, N.J.: Allyn and Bacon, 1978.

Wilson, G. B. Parents and Teachers: Humanistic Educational Technique to Facilitate Communication Between Parent and Staff of Child Development Centers. Atlanta, Ga.: Humanics, 1974.

Print Resources for Parents—Books

Baldwin, V. L., Fredericks, H., and Brodsky, G. Isn't It Time He Outgrew This? Or, a Training Program for Parents of Retarded Children. Springfield, Ill.: Charles C. Thomas, 1976.

Bannatyne, A., and Bannatyne, M. How Your Children Can Learn to Live a Rewarding Life: Behavioral Modification for Parents and Teachers. Springfield, Ill.: Charles C. Thomas, 1973.

Bateman, B. So You're Going to Hearing. Northbrook, Ill.: Hubbard, 1979.

Becker, W. C. Parents Are Teachers: A Child Management Program. Champaign, Ill.: Research Press, 1971.

Belton, S., and Terbough, C. Sparks: Activities to Help Children Learn at Home. New York: Human Sciences Press, (no date).

Brehm, S. S. Help for Your Child: A Parent's Guide to Mental Health Services. Englewood Cliffs, N.J.: Prentice-Hall, 1978.

Brown, D. L. Developmental Handicaps in Babies and Young Children: A Guide for Parents. Springfield, Ill.: Charles C. Thomas, 1972.

Brutten, M., Richardson, S. D., and Mangel, C. Something's Wrong with My Child: A Parents' Book About Children with Learning Disabilities. New York: Harcourt, Brace, Jovanovich, 1973.

Chalfant, J. C., and Van Dusen Pysh, M. The Compliance Manual: A Guide To the Rules and Regulations of P.L. 94-142. New Rochelle, N.Y.: Pathescope Educational Media, 1980.

Dorward, B. Teaching Aids and Toys for Handicapped Children. Reston, Va.: Council for Exceptional Children, 1960.

Evans, J. How to Fill Your Toyshelves Without Emptying Your Pocketbook: 70 Inexpensive Things to Do or Make. Reston, Va.: Council for Exceptional Children, 1976.

Fennie, N. R. Handling the Young Cerebral Palsied Child at Home. New York: E. P. Dutton, 1975.

Freeman, S. Does Your Child Have a Learning Disability? Springfield, Ill.: Charles C. Thomas, 1974.

Gardner, R. A. MBD: The Family Book about Minimal Brain Dysfunction. Part One: For Parents. Part Two: For Boys and Girls. New York: Jason Aronson, 1973.

Gordon, S., and Wollin, M. McD. Parenting: A Guide for Young People. New York: Oxford Book Co., 1975.

Gosciewski, F. W. Effective Child Rearing: The Behaviorally Aware Parent. New York: Human Sciences Press, 1976.

Hanson, M. Teaching Your Down's Syndrome Infant. Baltimore: University Park Press, 1978.

Heisler, V. A Handicapped Child in the Family: A Guide for Parents. New York: Grune and Stratton, 1972.

Help for Parents of Handicapped Children. King of Prussia, Pa.: Eastern Pennsylvania Regional Resources Center for Special Education and Pennsylvania Resources and Information Center for Special Education (no date).

Helping the Handicapped Through Parent/Professional Partnerships. Niles, Ill.: Developmental Learning Materials (no date).

Hersey, P., and Blanchard, K. H. The Family Game: A Situational Approach to Effective Parenting. Reading, Mass.: Addison-Wesley, 1978.

Hewett, S., and Newson, J. The Family and the Handicapped. Chicago: Aldine Press, 1970.

Isaacs, S. Troubles of Children and Parents. New York: Schocken Books, 1973.

Jenkins, J. K., and MacDonald, P. Growing Up Equal: Activities and Resources for Parents and Teachers of Young Children. Englewood Cliffs, N.J.: Prentice-Hall, 1979.

Karnes, M. B. Learning Language at Home. Reston, Va.: Council for Exceptional Children, 1977.

Kaufman, F. Your Gifted Child and You. Reston, Va.: Council for Exceptional Children, 1977.

Kozloff, M. A. A Program for Families of Children with Learning and Behavior Problems. New York: John Wiley & Sons, 1979.

Kozloff, M. A. Reaching the Autistic Child: A Parent Training Program. Champaign, Ill.: Research Press, 1973.

Kroth, R. Communicating with Parents of Exceptional Children: Improving Parent Teacher Relationships. Denver, Col.: Love Publishing, 1975.

Leitch, S. M. A Child Learns to Speak: A Guide for Parents and Teachers of Preschool Children. Springfield, Ill.: Charles C. Thomas, 1977.

Linde, T. F., and Kopp, T. Training Retarded Babies and Preschoolers. Springfield, Ill.: Charles C. Thomas, 1974.

Love, H. D. The Emotionally Disturbed Child: A Parents' Guide for Parents Who Have Problem Children. Springfield, Ill.: Charles C. Thomas, 1970.

Love, H. D. Parental Attitudes Toward Exceptional Children. Springfield, Ill.: Charles C. Thomas, 1970

Madsen, C. K., and Madsen, C. H., Jr. Parents and Children Love and Discipline: A Positive Approach to Behavior Modification. Arlington Heights, Ill.: AHM Publishing Corp., 1975.

Millman, J., and Behrmann, P. Parents as Playmates: A Games Approach to the Preschool Years. New York: Human Sciences Press, 1979.

Mopsik, S. I., and Agard, J. A. An Education Handbook for Parents of Handicapped Children. Cambridge, Mass.: Abt Associates, 1979.

Newman, S. Guidelines to Parent-Teacher Cooperation in Early Childhood Education. New York: Book-Lab, Inc., 1972.

Perske, R., and Perske, M. New Directions for Parents of Persons Who Are Retarded. Nashville, Tenn.: Abingdon Press, 1973.

Pope, L. Learning Disabilities Glossary. New York: Book-Lab, Inc., 1976.

Riley, M. T. LATON: The Parent Book. Atlanta, Ga.: Humanics, 1978.

Schachter, F. F. Everyday Mother Talk to Toddlers: Early Intervention. New York: Academic Press, 1979.

Sparling, J., and Lewis, I. Learning Games for the First Three Years: A Guide to Parent-Child Play. New York: Walker and Company, 1979.

Toys for Early Development of the Young Blind Child: A Guide for Parents. Illinois State Office of Superintendent of Public Information. Washington, D.C.: U.S. Department of Health, Education, and Welfare, Office of Education, 1971. (ERIC Document No. ED 065-201)

Turnbull, A., and Turnbull, H. R. Parents Speak Out: Views from the Other Side of the Two-way Mirror. Columbus, Ohio: Charles E. Merrill, 1978.

Wender, P. H. The Hyperactive Child—A Handbook for Parents. New York: Crown Publishers, 1973.

Wentworth, E. H. Listen to Your Heart: A Message to Parents of Handicapped Children. Boston: Houghton Mifflin, 1974.

Wiegerink, R., Posante, R., Bristol, M., and Hocutt, A. Parent Involvement in Early Education for Handicapped Children: A Review. Chapel Hill, N.C.: UNC Carolina Institute for Research on Early Education of the Handicapped, 1978.

Wing, L. Autistic Children: A Guide for Parents. New York: Brunner/Mazel, 1972.

Wolfensberger, W., and Zauha, H. Citizen Advocacy and Protective Services for the Impaired and Handicapped. Toronto: National Institute on Mental Retardation, 1973.

Other Print Resources for Parents

Pamphlets

Bijou, S. W. The Mentally Retarded Child. No. 20-5. 16 pages, $.25.
Order from: National Association for Retarded Citizens
2709 Avenue E East, P.O. Box 6109, Arlington, TX 76011.

Blanton, E. A Helpful Guide in the Training of a Mentally Retarded Child.
No. 20-2. 32 pages, $.50.
Order from: National Association for Retarded Citizens
2709 Avenue E East, P.O. Box 6109, Arlington, TX 76011.

The Blind Child: Is Your Child Blind? Shows parents how blind children develop and grow, and how parents can help them achieve maximum potential.
Order from: American Foundation for the Blind
15 West 16th Street, New York, NY 10011.

The Blind Child: The Preschool Deaf Blind Child. Gives suggestions to parents
for helping their deaf-blind child to learn to walk, eat, dress themselves, and accomplish other details of everyday living.
Order from: American Foundation for the Blind
15 West 16th Street, New York, NY 10011.

Dolye, P. B., Gotsky, J. N. et al. How to Help Your Child: A Guide for Parents
of Multiply Handicapped Children.
Order from: Montgomery County Intermediate Unit, Special Education
Center,
1605 B West Main Street, Norristown, Pennsylvania 19401.

Dybwad, G. The Mentally Handicapped Child Under Five. No. 10-10.
20 pages, $.25.
Order from: National Association for Retarded Citizens
2709 Avenue E East, P.O. Box 6109, Arlington, TX 76011.

First Aid Flip Chart. Fast assistance for medical emergencies. $2.00 plus
postage and handling.
Order from: The Ohio State University, The Nisonger Center,
McCampbell Hall, 1580 Cannon Drive, Columbus, OH 43210.

Gendel, E. S. Sex Education of the Mentally Retarded Child in the Home.
No. 30-11. 12 pages, $.30.
Order from: National Association for Retarded Citizens
2709 Avenue E East, P.O. Box 6109, Arlington, TX 76011.

Home Guide of Arts and Activities for Preschool Hearing-Impaired Children
     & Others. Describes activities parents can use to encourage mental,
     physical, and creative growth.
     Order from: National Easter Seal Society
     2023 West Ogden Avenue, Chicago, IL 60612.

Infant Stimulation Curriculum. Developmental norms—birth to 36 months, on
     cards. $11.50 plus postage and handling.
     Order from: The Ohio State University, The Nisonger Center
     McCampbell Hall, 1580 Cannon Drive, Columbus, OH 43210.

Infant Stimulation Curriculum Assessment Tool. Tool for assessing milestones
     in Infant Stimulation Curriculum. $3.00 plus postage and handling.
     Order from: The Ohio State University, The Nisonger Center
     McCampbell Hall, 1580 Cannon Drive, Columbus, OH 43210.

Klein, J. Teaching the Special Child in Regular Classrooms. Cat. #158.
     $2.00, 33 pages
     Order from: Publications Office, ERIC/ECE, University of Illinois
     805 West Pennsylvania Avenue, Urbana, IL 61801.

Meisels, S. J. Developmental Screening in Early Childhood: A Guide. $2.50.
     Available from: NAEYC, 1834 Connecticut Avenue, N.W.
     Washington, DC 20009.

Murray, M. A. Needs of Parents of Mentally Retarded Children. No. 65-3.
     16 pages, $.25.
     Order from: National Association for Retarded Citizens
     2709 Avenue E East, P.O. Box 6109, Arlington, TX 76011.

Perske, R. A. New Directions for Parents of Persons Who Are Retarded.
     No. 10-25. 64 pages, $1.95.
     Order from: National Association for Retarded Citizens
     2709 Avenue E East, P.O. Box 6109, Arlington, TX 76011.

Pitt, D. Your Down's Syndrome Child. No. 10-22. 32 pages, free.
     Order from: National Association for Retarded Citizens
     2709 Avenue E East, P.O. Box 6109, Arlington, TX 76011.

Practical Advice to Parents: A Guide to Finding Help for Handicapped Children
     & Youth. Discusses steps to take when problems are suspected, what to
     look for in school selection, financial aids, and parental attitudes.
     Order from: National Information Center for the Handicapped
     P.O. Box 1492, Washington, DC 20013.

Selected Reading Suggestions for Parents of Mentally Retarded Children.
     No. 10-15. 20 pages, $.40.
     Order from: National Association for Retarded Citizens
     2709 Avenue E East, P.O. Box 6109, Arlington, TX 76011.

Stabler, E. M. <u>Primer for Parents of a Mentally Retarded Child</u>. No. 10-12.
   18 pages, $.25.
   Order from: National Association for Retarded Citizens
   2709 Avenue E East, P.O. Box 6109, Arlington, TX 76011.

Stimson, C. W. <u>Understanding the Mongoloid Child</u>. No. 10-18. 12 pages, $.24.
   Order from: Association for Retarded Citizens
   2709 Avenue E East, P.O. Box 6109, Arlington, TX 76011.

Weskowitz, C. H. <u>The Parents of Retarded Children Speak for Themselves</u>.
   No. 30-6. 16 pages, $.40.
   Order from: National Association for Retarded Citizens
   2709 Avenue E East, P.O. Box 6109, Arlington, TX 76011.

Magazines

<u>The Exceptional Parent</u>
   P.O. Box 4944, Manchester, NH 03108

<u>School and Parent Digest</u>
   P.O. Box 1127, Newark, DE 19711

Books for Children

Preschool and Primary Grades

Aimar, C. <u>Waymond the Whale</u>. Illustrated by Martha Linder Heath.
    Englewood Cliffs, N.J.: Prentice-Hall, 1975.

Blue, R. <u>Me and Einstein: Break Through the Reading Barrier</u>. Illustrated by
    Peggy Luks. New York: Human Science Press, 1979.

Brightman, A. <u>Like Me</u>. Boston: Little, Brown, 1976.

Fanshawe, E. <u>Rachel</u>. Illustrated by Michael Charlton. Scarsdale, N.Y.:
    Bradbury, 1977.

Fassler, J. <u>Boy with a Problem</u>. Illustrated by Stuart Kranz. New York: Human
    Science Press, 1971.

Fassler, J. <u>Howie Helps Himself</u>. Illustrated by Joe Lasker. Chicago: Whitman,
    1975.

Fassler, J. <u>One Little Girl</u>. Illustrated by M. Jane Smith. New York: Human
    Science Press, 1969.

Goldfeder, C., and Goldfeder, J. <u>The Girl Who Wouldn't Talk</u>. Illustrated by
    Cheryl Goldfeder. Silver Spring, Md.: National Association of the
    Deaf, 1974.

Heide, F. <u>Sound of Sunshine, Sound of Rain</u>. New York: Parents' Magazine
    Press, 1970.

Hodges, E. J. <u>Free as a Frog</u>. Illustrated by Paul Giovanopoulos. Reading,
    Mass.: Addison-Wesley, 1969.

Krasilovsky, P. <u>The Shy Little Girl</u>. Illustrated by Trina Schart Hyman.
    Boston: Houghton Mifflin, 1972.

Kraus, R. <u>Leo the Late Bloomer</u>. Illustrated by Jose Aruego. New York:
    Dutton, 1973.

Lasker, J. <u>He's My Brother</u>. Illustrated by author. Chicago: A. Whitman, 1974.

Levine, E. S. <u>Lisa and Her Soundless World</u>. Illustrated by Gloria Kamen.
    New York: Human Sciences Press, 1974.

Litchfield, A. B. A Button in Her Ear. Pictures by Eleanor Mill. Chicago: A. Whitman, 1976.

Madsen, J., and Bockoras, D. Please Don't Tease Me. . . . Illustrated by Kathleen T. Brinko. Valley Forge, Pa.: Judson Press, 1980.

Peter, D. Claire and Emma. Photographs by Jeremy Finlay. New York: John Day, 1977.

Peterson, J. W. I Have a Sister, My Sister Is Deaf. Illustrated by Deborah Ray. New York: Harper and Row, 1977.

Peterson, P. Sally Can't See. New York: John Day, 1974.

Rogers, F. Danny's Song. Northbrook, Ill.: Hubbard, 1979.

Rogers, F. Josephine, the Short-neck Giraffe. Northbrook, Ill.: Hubbard, 1979.

Rogers, F. A Piece of Red Paper. Northbrook, Ill.: Hubbard, 1979.

Rogers, F. Speedy Delivery. Northbrook, Ill.: Hubbard, 1979.

Rogers, F. Who Am I? Northbrook, Ill.: Hubbard, 1979.

Simon, N. I Was So Mad! Pictures by Dora Leder. Chicago: A. Whitman, 1974.

Simon, N. Why Am I So Different? Illustrations by Dora Leder. Edison, N.J.: Gryphon House, 1979.

Sobol, H. L. My Brother Steven Is Retarded. Photographs by Patricia Ayre. New York: Macmillan, 1977.

Stanek, M. Left, Right, Left, Right. Pictures by Lucy Hawkinson. Chicago: A. Whitman, 1969.

Stein, S. B. About Handicaps: An Open Family Book for Parents and Children Together. Photographs by Dick Frank. New York: Walker, 1974.

Wolf, B. Anna's Silent World. Philadelphia: Lippincott, 1977.

Wolf, B. Don't Feel Sorry for Paul. Philadelphia: Lippincott, 1974.

Yashima, T. Crow Boy. New York: Viking Press, 1955.

Middle Grades

Baker, M. J. The Sand Bird. Illustrated by Floyd Garet. Nashville, Tenn.:
    Nelson, 1973.

Branfield, J. Why Me? New York: Harper and Row, 1973.

Bunting, E. One More Flight. Illustrated by Diane de Groat. New York:
    Warne, 1976.

Carper, L. D. A Cry in the Wind. Independence, Mo.: Herald, 1973.

Christopher, M. Stranded. Illustrated by Gail Owens. Boston: Little,
    Brown, 1974.

Corcoran, B. A Dance to Still Music. New York: Atheneum, 1974.

Courlander, H. The Son of the Leopard. Illustrated by Rocco Negri. New York:
    Crown, 1974.

de Angeli, M. Door in the Wall: Story of Medieval London. New York: Doubleday,
    1949.

First, J. Flat on My Face. New York: Avon Books, 1975.

Forbes, E. Johnny Tremain. Illustrated by Lynn Ward. Boston: Houghton Mifflin,
    1943.

Gill, D. L. Tom Sullivan's Adventures in Darkness. New York: McKay, 1976.

Gold, P. Please Don't Say Hello. Photographs by Carl Baker. New York: Human
    Sciences Press, 1975.

Leggett, L., & Andrews, L. The Rose-colored Glasses. Illustrated by Laura
    Hartman. New York: Human Sciences Press, 1979.

MacIntyre, E. The Purple Mouse. Nashville, Tenn.: Nelson, 1975.

Smith, D. B. Kelly's Creek. Illustrated by Alan Tiegreen. New York:
    Crowell, 1975.

Tate, J. Ben and Annie. Illustrated by Judith Gwyn Brown. Garden City, N.Y.:
    Doubleday, 1974.

Taylor, T. Teetoncey. Illustrated by Richard Cuffari. Garden City, N.Y.:
    Doubleday, 1974.

Wolf, B. Connie's New Eyes. Philadelphia: Lippincott, 1976.

Yolen, J. The Transfigured Hart. Illustrated by Donna Diamond. New York: Crowell, 1975.

Young Adults

Allan, M. E. Ship of Danger. New York: Abelard-Schuman, 1974.

Blume, J. Deenie. Scarscale, N.Y.: Bradbury, 1973.

Brown, F. G. You're Somebody Special on a Horse. Chicago: A. Whitman, 1977.

Brown, R. The White Sparrow. New York: Seabury, 1975.

Butler, B. Gift of Gold. New York: Dodd, 1973.

Cavanna, B. Joyride. New York: Morrow, 1974.

Christopher, M. Glue Fingers. Illustrated by Jim Venable. Boston: Little, Brown, 1975.

Cleaver, V., and Cleaver, B. Me Too. Philadelphia: Lippincott, 1973.

Corcoran, B. A Dance to Still Music. Illustrated by Charles Robinson. New York, Atheneum, 1974.

Davies, P. Fly Away Paul. New York: Crown, 1974.

Griffiths, H. The Mysterious Appearance of Agnes. Illustrated by Victor Ambrus. New York: Holiday House, 1975.

Grohskopf, B. Shadow in the Sun. New York: Atheneum, 1975.

Harnishfeger, L. Prisoner of the Mound Builders. Illustrated by George Overlie. Minneapolis, Minn.: Lerner, 1973.

Hunter, M. The Stronghold. New York: Harper and Row, 1974.

Lawrence, M. The Touchmark. Illustrated by Diane Hollinger. New York: Harcourt Brace Jovanovich, 1975.

Levine, B. A Griffon's Nest. New York: Macmillan, 1975.

Levine, E. S. Lisa and Her Soundless World. Illustrated by Gloria Kamen. New York: Human Sciences Press, 1974.

Mathis, S. B. _Listen for the Fig Tree_. New York: Viking Press, 1974.

McCracken, M. _Lovey: A Very Special Child_. Philadelphia: Lippincott, 1976.

Oppenheimer, J. _On the Outside Looking In_. Chicago: Scholastic, 1973.

Paterson, K. _Of Nightingales That Weep_. Illustrated by Haru Wells. New York: T. Y. Crowell, 1974.

Richard, A. _Wings_. Boston: Little, Brown, 1974.

Rinaldo, D. L. _Dark Dreams_. New York: Harper and Row, 1974.

Rodowski, C. F. _What about Me_? New York: Watts, 1976.

Savitz, H. M. _The Lionhearted_. New York: John V. Day, 1975.

Savitz, H. M. _On the Move_. New York: John V. Day, 1973.

Smith, G. _The Hayburners_. Illustrated by Ted Lewin. New York: Delacorte, 1974.

Swarthout, G., and Swarthout, K. _Whales to See_. Illustrated by Paul Bacon. Garden City, N.Y.: Doubleday, 1975.

Terris, S. _Plague of Frogs_. Garden City, N.Y.: Doubleday, 1973.

Watson, S. _The Partisan_. New York: Macmillan, 1975.

Photo Credits

P. x: Courtesy of Association for Retarded Citizens.

P. 16:   Photo by Dick Brown; courtesy of Centre Daily Times.

P. 20:   Photo by Joseph Bodkin.

P. 57:   Courtesy of Association for Retarded Citizens

P. 106:   Courtesy of Easter Seal Society for Crippled Children and
          Adults of Pennsylvania.

P. 111:   Photo by Joseph Bodkin.

P. 126:   Used with permission of HDS/U.S. HHS.

P. 139:   Photo by Joseph Bodkin.

P. 152:   Photo by Joseph Bodkin.

P. 156:   Photo by Joseph Bodkin.